You Have No Choice

You Have No Choice

Lindsay

BG

The Book Guild Ltd.
Sussex, England

HO

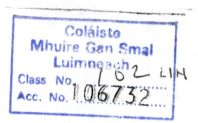
The Book Guild Ltd.
25 High Street,
Lewes, Sussex.

First published 1991
© Lindsay 1991
Set in Baskerville
Typesetting by APS,
Salisbury, Wiltshire.
Printed in Great Britain by
Antony Rowe Ltd.,
Chippenham, Wiltshire.
British Library Cataloguing in Publication Data
Lindsay
    You have no choice
    1. Philosophy
    I. Title
    100

ISBN 0 86332 557 2

Mum and Dad passed on to me the conscience of their forbears. I in turn have passed it on with as much love as I could muster to Tim and Jo. This book is dedicated with love to all my family.

Extract from a poem I found in Grandpa Hugh's writing.
So I sit alone with my conscience in the place where the years increase
And I try to remember the future in the land where time will cease
And I know of the future judgement how dreadful so e'er it be
That to sit alone with my conscience will be judgement enough for me.

AUTHOR'S NOTE

Reading this book could well change your well-ordered life. Despite yourself, and any initial rejection, you will find its truth insidiously intruding into your thoughts over the years. As you see the deep tragedies which are unfolding onto your own race, as you hear the views being expressed by expert or amateur alike, you will begin to question them, and, more importantly, you will begin questioning yourself. Watch out for those who seem to be continuing to live in the threatening shadow of their own well-ordered lives.

Regardless of what you now believe, regardless of your acceptance of what follows in these pages, the seed will have been planted from which the tree of truth will begin to grow. Let it!

1

My son was in his early teens when he asked me if there really was a God. I was touched that he loved me enough even to ask the question as well as by his faith in me to provide an answer. What he did not know was that his great grandfather, in the fashion of Victorian society, had spent much of his life looking for answers to similar questions.

My life too, as with many others of my era, had been guided by religious teachings which left chasms of doubt to any who were prepared to question them. Many were not because they had been taught that the religion was ordained by an all-powerful God who would cast any doubters into eternal hell and damnation. Many others denied his existence as the easiest way out of having to live to some sort of standard set by others. The answer I gave my son was, 'Yes', but not any God about which he had been taught.

I told him that he should accept the principles but reject the details of what had been put into his mind over the years by religious teachers. He should revel in what he had been given while he could, that is those things he could detect with the given senses of sight, hearing, smell, taste and touch as well as his own feelings and, as his life progressed, the rest would follow.

But now I see that was not enough. For the beauty of the world has become shrouded in an invisible mist of hate, violence, horror and fear which the inhabitants of this planet are doing little to disperse and indeed it is becoming the accepted norm by many. Unless this creeping terror is recognized and purged it will slowly but inexorably lead to the end of humanity. Whatever religion or God you believe in, do not expect eternal life to be a refuge to which you can turn, for without the continuation of Man it does not exist.

All of us, no matter how caring we think we are, are guilty of allowing millions of people to die of malnutrition, curable illnesses and terror. Our power lies within our declared democracy where we can demand that our rulers make us collectively responsible for those less fortunate than ourselves. Terror too we allow to run freely whether it is in ignoring the wholesale genocide which is taking place across the world or in not tackling the problems of violence in our own streets and cities. Thus the behaviour of a few mindless, indeed psychopathic in some cases, fellow human beings is allowed to rule the lives of thousands of millions of people by fear, with governments either unable or unwilling to do anything to stop them.

Only after the event does our anger bring the need to satiate our natural emotions by hateful revenge. Too many, far, far too many people use the human rights cause to produce ineffective laws. These in turn cause frustration, anger and mistrust against those who have the often impossible job of protecting the innocent. Mistrust of police forces prompts even less effective laws and sometimes regrettably pushes law officers, frustrated at their inability to see justice is done, to override them. The way ahead is anarchy unless we, the silent majority, are prepared to force drastic changes to protect the vulnerable people of the world. Our failure will only lead to greater terror with the strong possibility of a backlash in some form of vigilante mob rule. History is littered with such actions and reactions.

The goal, one that Man has professed to seek throughout the ages, is simply that all people of the world can live free from fear. That must mean, at the very least, that the better off look after the poor and protect the weaker members of our societies – wives, children, grown up daughters and elderly relatives (which I, and you, will rapidly become) so that they may walk about the streets, or the countryside, or rest unmolested inside their own homes without fear of attack or death. That is not too much to ask and indeed we must demand it as the minimum right of every person on this planet, from those organizations supposedly interested in individual freedom, from all members of the human race and particularly from those who want to govern. Forget religion, forget colour, forget your insulated lives and become involved in making a secure future for your race.

This is not another fashionable 'green' lobby nor yet an

appeal on behalf of other forms of life; this is about the future of the human race. How much longer can the better-off nations cosset themselves, ignoring the pitiful despair of fellow humans who, through no fault of their own, are dying in their millions from hunger or suffering indescribable horrors in the grip of unwinnable, stupid, pointless civil wars. Can we, as individuals, really live behind the shrug of helplessness and do nothing except cast a few crumbs across to them from time to time?

The two superpowers of late Twentieth Century can claim a major part in the continuation of the senseless slaughter of helpless people. Their individual self interest, mistrust and established dogma has brought them so often to the brink of war. We must thank the nuclear arsenals that most of us escaped the horrors of another war. We must blame the same weapons for the stalemate which has involved proxy wars with either one side or the other propping up regimes of killers and thieves. The demi-superpowers too cannot escape blame, wrapped in their own national problems, avoiding any comment or action which may affect their standing with their related superpower.

The problem is that Man's disgust at the depths of degradation to which his fellow Man has sunk, coupled with the mistrust which has been festered in those people on which he had come to rely, has destroyed his faith in any human being outside his own small circle of family, friends or acquaintances. What a tragedy that is, for distrust eats away the fabric of life and causes us to spurn even the good Samaritan.

Like me I expect you regularly hear about the work of the thousands of international organizations whose objectives vary from the protection of the environment and the world's wildlife to the protection of human rights, each organization having its own interpretation of what is important. I hear and see daily, outcry after outcry against Man's apparent disregard for the world's animals and plant life or against alleged infringement of human rights. Many organizations are helping in the battle against hunger, thirst and disease. All are doing all they can but, through no fault of their own, it is not enough. More resources are needed. But there seems to be a lack of any cohesive organization that is taking action on behalf of the massive and gross inhuman disregard of humans. Where are the governments of the world? Where are the political leaders who can together forge powerful world laws in the interest of every individual on earth? We the people must begin to recognize that we have to make some sacrifices now to regain our freedom from fear and we must look for politicians whose objectives are totally based on a philosophy of Life First. This would mean that all their actions would be aimed at the protection and enrichment of all human life regardless of nationality or beliefs.

The Green Party began a move in the direction of protection of the planet with other political parties jumping on the band wagon as they realized the power of the voter. But we need to go further, not only to protect our environment but to protect man as a species. With political parties of every colour having an input into this philosophy, a white Party would be appropriate as the only colour which contains the spectrum of all the other colours within it.

It is of little use saving the planet whilst people are allowed to die from lack of interest or while fear is permitted to run people's lives. We need an honest appraisal of what is happening on our planet and we need scheduled plans of action to help those unable to help themselves. Of top priority is the need to stop, and reverse as quickly as possible, the growing trend of unacceptably violent behaviour either by groups or individuals. Sod politics! Any government leader working towards the needs of the world's human race should be supported by those who can better afford to do so. If some human acts are actually, not theoretically, affecting the globe then, in the interests of our future, such acts must cease and compensation paid to those affected. Is any price too high if the planet's ability to support life is threatened?

How can any sane person justify what is going on in Europe at present where farmers are paid not to produce food while millions of other human beings are starving to death in countries ravaged by Man and Nature? Obscene is not sufficiently derogatory to describe this policy which we, yes you and I, are condoning by our apathy. Something can be done but we need caring leaders to take us where we want to go.

It is no use shutting our eyes to the problems or arguing that things are not deteriorating or are too far away to affect our lifestyle. Individual's lives, indeed all forms of life on this planet, are under threat. So let us humans in the richer nations, or those in the poorer whose main occupation is not simply surviving the next day, pause a while from the comparative megalomania which drives us and consider our future. God help us, we are the only, and thus the most, intelligent beings we know!

He came, he breathed, he died. Thus sums up the infinitesimal time in earth's history every individual member of the human race, whether still-born or living for over one hundred years, spends on this planet. Why he is here and what is his purpose in life are two of the fundamental questions which, at some time during that short stay and in one form or another, plagues all of us.

What we do not yet seem to have come to terms with is that every individual member of the race differs from all others around him, in thought, in action, in reaction and in trying to establish what he wants from life. We try to draw up codes of behaviour, some important, many irrelevant, and scorn and punish those who are unable to achieve them. But even those who are not found out in their code breaking have to calm the nagging fundamental questions by throwing themselves into activities to occupy their lives, if possible those from which they derive the greatest pleasure. It is not until death has stared them personally in the face that they begin to re-examine the priorities on which they have based their lives and, perhaps for the first time ever, begin to see them for what they really were – unimportant, insignificant and trivial.

For some there is no escape and they are forced to consider the reasons for their life in a world in which they appear to have no role. They begin to search through the recesses of their minds for any tiny specks of understanding which may have been placed there by others or may have developed from their own experiences. Often such specks evolve into the pursuit of a neglected God whose advocates on earth can provide the sustenance needed by the weary soul. But not always. For while it is true to say that unquestioning faith does help many of those individuals who need it, it is only the confused, tired or frightened minds that reject the thoughts and doubts about the religious beliefs which their societies have thrust upon them.

But for all of us death is inevitable and no-one can escape. And as it approaches it becomes necessary for the living to give as much comfort and support as they can both to those who can no longer be kept alive by medical science and those who remain to mourn. In today's world, in many societies, this simply means easing the pain and fear as death approaches and being unable to find ways of expressing our feelings to the bereaved. But in other societies, even today, there are millions upon millions of people who are being forced to unmourned painful deaths by fellow Man while others allow it to happen, watching the tragedies with horror but seemingly unable to help. The victims feel deserted by God and Man alike, left devoid of any feelings, hopelessly knowing they will not get the help which could sometimes be easily given. Their deaths, and indeed their lives, and those of their families and friends are always without dignity or comfort to ease the extraordinary pain which surrounds them. Do we care? And if we do, what are we doing about it?

Looking back at this Twentieth Century as it draws to a close we can see that there is virtually no person in the world who was born in the first half whose life has not been dramatically affected by changes. In the so-called developed countries, for example, advances in medical sciences have eradicated a number of the illnesses and diseases to which many lost friends or relatives in the first half of the century. Sadly however those diseases, thankfully unknown to present generations of developed countries, continue to ravage and kill in all the under-developed countries of the world. This is another preventable tragedy which decimates the survival of the poor people of the world. Worse, they are further dehumanized by the twin malignant horrors of tyranny and war. Relief from torture, illness, slaughter, untreated wounds and the pangs of starvation comes only with death itself and the pain which precedes such relief is a suffering that no human being should, under any circumstances whatsoever, allow to happen to another. Charity is not enough. We can, we must, do more.

Scientific progress, ironically speeded up by two world wars, has also dramatically changed Man's perception of himself and his world, both individually and collectively. The arrival of the new mass media of radio and television has enabled him to be presented with a wider sphere of thoughts and ideas than was available to his ancestors of the Nineteenth Century. It has enabled him to become more aware of what is going on on his own planet beyond his previously limited geographical location. He has begun to look beyond his own planet, launched himself into space, visited the moon and has sent exploratory unmanned craft into the far reaches of space in an endeavour to find out more about the creation of the universe itself. All such work is ultimately geared to his search for answers to the fundamental question, his own origins and destinies. His greater knowledge has simply highlighted his long held doubts that there must be more to life than the beliefs that have been passed down to him, beliefs set out hundreds of years ago by his less enlightened ancestors. The serious doubts in his mind about the teachings, that Man is the only intelligent being created by God, have increased with his knowledge. As he looks at what is happening in his own world those doubts explode into incredulity as he sees the unspeakable horrors being committed by his own race. He cannot reconcile how the kind and loving God about whom he had been taught could ever have created such hideous monsters.

Despite massive strides in his learning and understanding Man has failed, being unable or unwilling, to find a solution about how to bring peace and love to his own tiny world. Indeed it is because of that failure that a dislike of his fellow Man has developed and is growing. Anger has given way to hatred and violence against great masses of people who are seen in a globally collective way as corrupt and devoid of any of the higher human feelings of love, tenderness, understanding and sympathy. So breeds intolerance.

Thus, as the century moves to its close, wars and terrorism continue unabated, growing progressively more vicious, more cruel, more sick, with many leaders and their followers wallowing in a sadism which brings yet more millions of deaths to innocent people. A small flame of hope burns very faintly in the ashes of disastrous wars but many parts of the world have yet to notice it and it needs fanning or it will die. It is up to the more affluent nations to provide the fan. You, and me.

And all over the world human life becomes daily more cheap. Fears of all sorts are curbing Man's normal life, affecting his freedom in a big way. Thus a basic human right, the freedom to live without fear, is denied to all vulnerable people which includes the majority of us. People from all generations in every nation are crying out for leaders to act, rather than talk, to reverse the downward spiral into which Mankind is being sucked. But, in the politics of the world, where success is measured in material wealth, governments look towards the needs of the moment rather than tackling the major world problems. Yet they are threatening the very future of Mankind. The result of this philosophy is that material wealth has become the yardstick against which individuals measure their own success in life as well as that of those around them. Despite the rumbling consciences of those of us that have food, clothing and shelter, we are able to satisfy ourselves that there is little or nothing that we can do on our own to solve such massive problems except to provide some financial help from time to time. Not enough to hurt but enough to salve a nagging conscience. I do, do you?

What the hell! In less than one hundred and fifty years from now every person currently living on this planet will be dead so the question arises about the futility of worrying too much about the future of the world. After all there are enough problems of today on their own doorsteps to keep nations occupied for many years. But local problems become national and then world problems and to continue to ignore them will mean gambling with the future of Mankind. To concede that there is nothing to be done will mean its downfall. Do you care what happens to the world after you have gone? Should you? We need to look back at what is it that shapes our attitudes.

For many centuries Man's thinking, his laws and his societies, have been guided by religious leaders and in the 1990s they continue to play a major role in the actions of nations, too often regrettably to the detriment of the world's inhabitants. But the churches of all beliefs, once the leaders in education, have failed to update their pedantic adherence to teachings derived from written words, even though the meanings they have put on them may have been overtaken by Man's growing knowledge. Consequently, in many countries, religions are struggling to survive or have been replaced by a fanaticism which will destroy them. When faced with the massive human tragedies all over the world they seem impotent and present an image which, to many, seems to resort to primitive practices like lighting candles whilst praying to a God who does not seem to hear or care.

In a world of senseless violence the simplistic explanation to

14

grief-stricken people, who desperately need to know why a loved one was prematurely taken from them, that God was watching it all happen and his inactivity was simply to test the faith of the afflicted, is no longer adequate. Nor can they readily accept the promises, that no human can truly make anyway, that provided they maintain their faith God will, in due time, reward them, if not in this life then in the next. Such an almost arrogant attitude can be compared to those individual religions or denominations which have too much faith, believing that everything that happens to them is the will of God, and they thus deny their children life-saving operations, blood transfusions, vaccinations or other medicines, allowing them to die if necessary. Or perhaps compared to suttee, where Hindu widows threw themselves on the funeral pyres of their dead husbands as part of their faith. While the British were in India they fought long and hard to stop what was, to them, a barbaric practice. Today it is no longer acceptable in most parts though it was widespread at the beginning of the century and society condemns the faith of those parents who believe in the will of God and deny their children any life-saving medical aids.

Nor has Man yet accepted that the world belongs to him and he cannot stand by watching it deteriorate waiting for God to put it right. Even within religions the all powerful God is seen as a father figure and as such he will be expecting his children to do something for themselves to solve their own problems, particularly those which they themselves had created. But both politics and religions are controlled by vested interests of one sort or another and each are afraid of changes which may adversely affect the power of their leaders, for it is from them that they themselves derive power. In many of the world's faiths the consequences of Man's questioning can be seen, as over the centuries, dissident groups have split off to establish differing beliefs and practices within the same religion. The pontification by the churches of their differing religions and their inflexible defence of those beliefs and doctrines which they had been taught, despite the fact that they are doing little or nothing to improve the state of the world, makes them seem out of touch with the realities that are facing mankind.

They have failed to give a modern and more understandable lead to their followers and this has resulted not only in a loss of

15

many of those followers but, worse, has cast serious concern in the minds of many millions of people who, though they still firmly believe in a God, are unable to see how the image of him that the churches present relates to the reality of what is happening around them.

The lack of direction has been replaced by religious fanaticisms where the followers give the adulation due to God to their spiritual leaders, laying down their lives with fervour for any whim which takes his fancy. Such religion bears no resemblance to the kind and loving world that was previously associated with God. The fear of God, which the church has fully used to its advantage in the struggle for power, has been overridden by a real fear which can be seen, touched and felt. This fear is growing with the anxiety that violence is inexorably taking control of the destiny of nations, while governments avoid involving themselves in any measures necessary to bring it to a halt.

But inaction will inevitably result in a fear-driven backlash which will carry in its wake a virtual breakdown in law and order. Such a backlash is only being delayed by fear itself. But the alternative is to allow the world to be ruled by ruthless tyrants who have no respect for life. Which ever way you look at it its not a great pair of alternatives, for either way the consequences for Mankind would be disastrous. Is this the legacy we want to leave for our children and their descendants? If we continue to keep our heads down and struggle through life we may be able to manage by active non-interference to avoid the mischance of personal violence and leave it for future generations to sort out.

Hope for a sane world diminishes even further when those carrying out terrible acts of violence justify it to themselves, and everyone else, as being the will of whatever God they worship. Yet often their sadism, which maims and kills indiscriminately, is aimed at those groups or nations with the same God but with different fundamental beliefs. Sometimes death is heaped upon a hated nation's citizens even though some may have exactly the same beliefs as the terrorist killers. And, tragically for our future, powerful nations lend succour to such carnage. In God's name there are no limits to the depths of horror to which Man can descend in venting his hatred against any fellow man who, even remotely, appears to him not to

16

support his cause. Death and destruction becomes the means regardless of whether the people involved (be they men, women or children) are, even in the blinkered vision of the terrorists, guilty or innocent. What is far worse is when such terrible violence is either openly encouraged, or not actively discouraged, by religious leaders who say they are speaking for the God who has chosen them to lead. The Thugs of India, who attacked and ceremoniously garrotted their victims as sacrifices to the Hindu goddess Kali, were declared Public Enemy Number One and were suppressed. So should any terror, inflicted in any God's name, be roundly condemned.

But such has been the fear of one nation for another that people who desperately want an end to the hatred and bloodshed do nothing but express revulsion from time to time at the horrors being committed. That fear had stemmed from the belief that to do otherwise may lead them into a war which they did not want and which could become even more devastating. Thus, unless they expected the horrors to affect them directly, no government would involve their nation in solving what they see as someone else's problems. The result has been stalemate inactivity which only feeds the unchecked flames of violence to greater and more horrific levels.

Even more inhumane in its scale are the cases of the millions of unfortunate men, women and children who are deliberately starved to death. Time after time massive funds have been donated by more fortunate but ordinary people from many nations who have been moved by the plight of those in need. Governments too, have helped and from all sources food, water, clothing and medical supplies have been provided. But tragically they could not be delivered because the agreement of the leaders of the factions who held sway over the land, sea and air routes would not be given, often simply because the starving people did not belong to the same religious sect as the faction leaders themselves.

The argument, often used, that the supplies could end up in the hands of rebels was simply an excuse to cover their inhumane actions. The powerful countries of the world should have vigorously condemned such behaviour as unacceptable in human terms and action taken. Any intelligent beings, or God himself, observing the world from the heavens would consider the rulers on this planet to be an inhumane, callous and uncaring lot. No wonder we don't think too highly of ourselves! It raises the question of what the observers would say about the rest of us who simply stood by and watched as millions of poor innocent wretches were, and still are today, left to die lingering deaths having seen their own children or parents die of starvation before them, their cries for help unheeded. How long can we continue to be sure that nothing can be done or is it that, like with so many other distasteful things around us, we pretend not to notice?

And is there any developed nation which can legitimately criticize such actions within the newer nations when similar hatred and bigotry have been nurtured over many centuries in their so-called civilized communities. It is not unknown for the latter to freely use the countries of the poorer nations as live testing grounds for the arsenal of new weapons of destruction which they are developing, even though they have often been too sophisticated for the peasant population that were using them.

The problem has been that the lack of any firm, active and single approach to life and its meaning has left a gaping void to all human beings on this planet. Many people, some well meaning, some simply power mad, have been trying to fill the gap in their own way but all too often have just added to the confusion. Violence has resulted, mindless and senseless. In individuals. In small groups. In whole communities. In nations. We have closed our eyes once too often to cut out what we do not want to see. Now our own personal lives are affected with a daily growing fear. And still there, behind the now growing concern for the escalation of violence in the world, lies the core of those fundamental questions which have beset every human mind in every generation but never one more knowledgeable or free thinking than today's. Religion has played a large part in much of the global violence of late which makes me, at least, wonder why. If Man really believed the religious teachings of the concept, that after three score years and ten of good behaviour on this earth he could look forward to an everlasting life of happiness, it is certainly not supported by his conduct. Somewhere along the way his beliefs have been hijacked, but how? Modern Man has found it difficult to conjure up what life after death would be like and can see little reason behind it, indeed it is seen by many in the same way as a parental ploy to children of promising rewards for good behaviour. But such a ploy will only work when the children see the promises fulfilled. Thus God could have all his commands obeyed to the letter by a simple demonstration of the rewards or punishments in the next life which his representatives keep promising.

But if the world denies immortality, or indeed the existence of God himself, what is there left to live for but one's own immediate pleasure and hang the rest of humanity and its future. There are growing signs that, in the absence of any confirmation that he has a future, Man is sliding slowly towards such an attitude and the Me First society is burgeoning. But for some inexplicable reason, which is fortunate for mankind, there remains within all of us some force which knows there is more to life than just today. So we cling to our concept of God, knowing nothing else and hoping all the time that he will save us. Deep down is the growing knowledge that it is a forlorn hope.

Man must take charge of his own destiny and to do that he must first look at the differing societies and the laws under which the peoples of the world live and see how they have built up over the years, based upon the religious beliefs which have been taught in their countries. Where there are two or more religions in one country, or where there are two or more sects of the same religion, there is conflict. In today's world such conflict surfaces in violent, bloody and vicious hate. No God, under any name given by Man, would reward those people who are exacting such a price from his fellows using his name. On the contrary they can expect his full wrath. If Mankind itself is to survive, and allow its members to lead reasonably happy lives, it is essential for all of us, right now as the key inhabitant of our planet, to make a start to loosen the restrictive and tight lines of the differing religious dogmas and to move towards uniting the human race as one body.

Unless the peoples of the world at large begin to look at the future of Man as a whole then that future becomes threatened or, at best, very grim indeed. The time is now to consider again why we are on earth and, with minds and hearts open, to seriously review whether the interpretations of the holy scriptures which have been taught to us for generations, and as set out in so many differing religions, are likely to help achieve a

19

happy future or destroy it. Enough people have used God, through the scriptures, to climb to power and maintain it regardless of the cost in human degradation. Forget politics, forget religion, forget, for a moment, yourself because your attitudes have been instilled into your life. Think of the world, think of the future and ask yourself if you have any part in that future.

2

In trying to understand our future we must accept that we have our limitations. We must recognize that, even with our knowledge today, we have hardly scratched the surface of what is going on around us and there are many, many things well beyond our present comprehension. We are unable, for example, to imagine limitless space or infinity, yet we accept them as fact. If, as individuals, we cannot accept limitless space and tried to think of it as limited, what could we imagine beyond those limits?

In looking forward we must first look back. The religious writings which have formed such a major part of the lives of most of us cannot be rejected as they all have some historical basis. But we cannot look at all the world's religions, which have differing scriptures generally divided into 'revelations', such as Christianity where Christ revealed the word of God, and 'natural' such as Buddhism which result from human speculation alone. Whatever the scripture there is an absolute need to look again at the interpretations placed upon them by our less enlightened forefathers who, in determining the approach to God, were constrained to make their interpretations acceptable to their times and within the limits of their understanding. Thus at times, when they found themselves unable to explain the written words of the scriptures, they invoked superstition and fear which was used to hold power and control society's actions. We cannot fault them for that. But throughout history there have been many religious leaders who have exercised power through the misuse of fear and many campaigns have been fought, and continue to be fought, in the name of God, under the banners of religious crusades. As we look at the scriptures it is of great importance to remember that they were written many years after the deaths of their religious creators, so we need to wonder how much of the writings were written by those with vested interests for power.

As an individual you will have to search through your own scriptures with a mind uncluttered by what you have been conditioned to see. It isn't easy, it's damned difficult, particularly for those of a deep faith in what they have been taught to believe. Often they have been taught by those they love dearly and feel that questioning their faith is rejecting their loved ones. Not true. You owe it to your children and, indeed, to the world's youngsters, as we need to fill an aching void in many of their lives. So, with an open mind, first consider the origins of the scriptures, that is who wrote them and when; who translated them into their language and when; who interpreted them and when; and finally are you satisfied that what has been impressed upon you and your ancestors for generations and which now forms the basis of your family's lives is important to their future as well as that of mankind as a whole? Look at particular inconsistencies between faiths. For example some religions ban alcohol, some smoking, while other faiths ban theatre, radio and television. Some ban eating pigs as unclean, others ban eating cows because they are sacred; yet others ban eating any meat at all; others have a similar ban, but only on Fridays. The differences are endless yet those people who need a God more than most are those who cannot get water to drink let alone any of the items banned in religious laws. Are such practices really important to the human race?

Christianity, which is the basic religion of my country, and is claimed to be the largest of the religions, is the one on which I will raise questions but similar questions can be made about every other religion or belief in the world. Remember Christianity itself arose from the Jewish faith which is based on the Old Testament of the Bible, a book recognized by most other religions at some time. It is essential for any review for each of us to set aside parochial or historical ideas and, for once in our lives, to consider Mankind as a whole. Above everything else the last thing that is needed is yet another religion or another faith. And I do not want to go deeply into Christianity but simply to look at those stories of which most of us are aware.

Everything we have been taught over the generations ostensibly comes from the Bible but the differences of interpretation can drive deep antagonistic wedges between those of the same faith, bringing religious bigotry, hatred and horrific deaths

22

over the centuries. For most of us who are not driven to make others die for our extremism in faith we find many troubling features in what we were taught and which continues to be taught to our children. The opening chapter of the Old Testament, for example, covers the creation of the world and Man himself and it immediately highlights one of the major questions that arises many times each year in the minds of those (including me) who wonder about themselves, their ancestors and their heirs. The mind searching often culminates in the most fundamental question of all which asks:

'Is there really a God at all?'

Christians are taught to believe that an omnipotent God placed Adam and Eve on a world he had created in six days. There Adam committed the sin of eating the forbidden fruit, taught to mean in the language of the 1980s that they had sex together, an action which God had built naturally into every other animal in his kingdom for, quite simply, without it there would be no life. As sex is necessary for the fertilisation of the egg in every other female on earth before they may have babies and thus continue the species, why then should Man think that God made male and female for any other reason? It makes me wonder if God really did forbid Adam to touch the fruit and if so why? In these days of sexual equality I sometimes wonder why God didn't forbid Eve to touch Adam's forbidden fruit; after all when it comes to sex it is women who drive the bus! Today however Man is aware that his world has evolved over many millions of years in a scientifically natural way. He now knows his own presence on this planet is very, very recent. There is a need therefore, in the light of his greater knowledge, to update the meanings expressed in the Bible and not retain those interpretations which were placed on the written word by our ancestors who did not have that knowledge.

Because Man is the most intelligent being on the planet he must make himself responsible for it. Regrettably his intelligence has brought with it one of Man's major problems, his arrogance which has built up over the centuries from those religious teachings which for many thousands of years placed earth as the centre of the universe, with himself as the pinnacle of God's creation. Yet there is absolutely nothing in this world of any substance which he has created or for which he can genuinely take credit. By his work he may, in his own eyes,

23

have used well or improved on those things already put on the planet, but their ability to last, to stand, to grow, are totally dependent on powers outside his own control and understanding. We know certain things we do work, but we do not know why. Man is able to perceive, as well as think, so that he can absorb beauty. Many painters and poets have tried to capture the beauty and awesome splendour of their world but because their medium is limited they have merely, though successfully, highlighted some of the planet's beauty in the very small window pane that they have captured. Many man-made structures, splendid on their own, do not even register as a tiny dot on the massive landscape which surrounds them. Yet Man prides himself on his creations and puts high material values on them. His selection of the Seven Wonders of the World were all his own creations.

Yet all peoples, rich or poor, can derive untold pleasure from natural creations such as breathtaking scenery, watching animals in their own environment, or simply enjoying the pleasure of a beautiful day. But enjoyment can only be had with the contentment of a full belly and the absence of fear. All animals given those two conditions would revel in the wonders of the planet. But Man's belief in his own importance stems from the words of the Old Testament of the Bible when God himself gave Man dominion over every living thing that moved on earth telling him that all life, both vegetable and animal, was there for his use. The lives of the animals thus became Man's for the taking and he did so to meet all his needs for food and clothing. But he also killed to make money, as in the whale meat and fur trades. He also killed to stop their natural activities affecting his pocket, as in seal culls or using disease to try to annihilate the rabbit 'nuisance'. He also killed simply to provide good sport or satisfy his lust for killing. And in this latter area Man indeed shines brilliantly, for his imagination has known no bounds when it comes to developing weapons of destruction or more sadistic methods of inflicting pain, distress and agony on both animals and fellow humans alike. Yet even in this area, despite committing a major part of the world's resources to developing and providing new killing devices, his weaponry is feeble when compared with the enormous power of even minor events which can be produced by Mother Nature.

Man's knowledge, even of his own planet, is very limited. The oceans' beds and, indeed, the waters themselves lay largely unexplored along with the major mass of the planet which lies underneath the earth's crust. And yet it is from beneath that crust, whose thickness has been described as being comparable to the skin of a bubble, that the countries of the world have evolved.

Thus hundreds of millions of years are condensed in a sentence at the beginning of the Old Testament which gives us no clues to the answers about the creation and development of the world. We are told that it was many millions of years after the earth was born that the planet's animals began to evolve and hundreds of more millions of years before Man himself made his appearance. One fact I found curious was the way the Bible, starting with Adam and Eve, sets out family trees which followed, presumably, the lifting of God's ban on the forbidden fruit. There are several paragraphs about who begat whom and it is interesting to contemplate why such genealogy was included.

But the Old Testament is far more important to the Jews who see Moses getting his commands from God. Christianity itself is based on the life of Christ as written in the four gospels of the New Testament of the Bible. These books cover events from his conception to birth, and, apart from a few references about his childhood, his activities and sermons during his short adult life up to his death and resurrection. The birth of Jesus is historically dated to about 2,000 years ago, an extremely short time even in Man's very limited time on earth, and very far removed from the creation of the world hundreds of millions of years earlier.

And in the New Testament we find in the first book of the gospels that genealogy appears again, with Matthew setting out the path from Abraham to Joseph the husband of Mary, of whom was born Jesus Christ. And we all know of the nativity scene but I cannot remember anyone telling me that Matthew recorded that Mary was due to marry Joseph, but before they came together, she was found with a child of the Holy Ghost. The new edition of the gospels says that Joseph was going to divorce Mary, but an angel which visited him in his dreams, talked him round. When he awoke he took Mary home and Matthew records that Joseph had no union with her until the baby was born. One wonders where Matthew got such intimate information! I also wonder how many people living at the time would have believed that it was not Joseph's child. How would we treat anyone telling such a story today?

And in his gospel Luke tells us that before Mary was visited, the angel Gabriel had visited Zechariah to tell him that his wife Elizabeth had been chosen to be the mother of John the Baptist. When old Zechariah expressed an opinion that his wife of advanced years was not capable of having a baby, Gabriel, who must have been unimpressed at what Zechariah had to say, struck him dumb until the baby was born.

There are many occasions throughout the gospels when the angels of the Lord made appearances and, from what we read, it seems that those specially selected for favours were unable to refuse them or even question them without some form of punishment. They were required to show the proper appreciation of the honour they had been given, or else!

Gabriel's tough approach to Zechariah did come in handy later on when he visited Mary, who Luke also recorded as a virgin pledged to marry Joseph, and told her that she was highly favoured with God and thus was to become pregnant. Even in today's world it does seem very hard on Mary. She seemed to think so too for she voiced her doubts but was referred to her relative Elizabeth. Following a visit Mary seemed to understand where she stood. The very fact that Zechariah and Joseph were told is because, somehow or another, the seeds of the child would have to be planted in the wombs of the wives. It clearly could not be done unknowingly or there would have been no reason to talk to the husband, or in Mary's case, the fiancé. It is interesting to contemplate how people of today would react if they were visited by an alien, or an apparition, or whatever, to be told they had been chosen for honours similar to those given (not offered) to Elizabeth and Mary. In both visits by the angel the parents were told the names the babies were to be given which meant that the sex of the children to be was known. Luke's book tells us that Zechariah got his voice back when, in answer to the neighbours and relatives disbelief that Elizabeth was to call him John, a name not known in the family, he wrote the name down.

Whichever way you look at it the whole episode seems extremely harsh on those who were supposed to be highly favoured. But then again the God in the Bible was, to say the least, very demanding. Throughout the Bible stories that most of us know God appears to have had little direct control over Man, his own creation, having to resort to threats and violence to get himself obeyed. Examples are where Adam ate of the forbidden fruit; Cain, his first born slew Abel his brother; then there was Sodom and Gommorrah and finally the flood in order that God could make a fresh start. I cannot see how God could count his creation of Man a success. On the other hand he does show his ability to wreak vengeance when he was displeased. How do these actions of major destruction compare with the picture of God as presented by the preachers of Christ's teachings, of a kind, loving and forgiving God? And if God were omnipotent and the creator of Adam and Eve why was it necessary to make Elizabeth and Mary pregnant?

Most of us know of the gospel story of the Magi coming in search of the King of the Jews after the birth of Christ. The Bible says that they were following a star which they had seen in the east which went ahead of them until it stopped over the place where the child was. A star? The nearest star, not counting the sun (though a lot of us like to follow that one) is seen from earth as it was four years ago since that is the time taken for the light to travel from the star to earth. The light from the most distant bodies yet photographed takes over one thousand million years to reach this planet – such time being another of those things beyond my comprehension. With light travelling at 186,000 miles per second the term 'astronomical' can be used here in its true meaning.

Come on people, any 'star' which was able to pin-point a small building like the stable in which Christ was born, or indeed one which could be seen to be moving slow enough across the sky to follow, would have to be close to the ground. We are aware, with today's knowledge, that any such body would burn up on entering the earth's atmosphere or its remains would crash with tremendous force into the ground. It would certainly not hover overhead and, even if it could, it would be of such an immense size that it could not help being extremely noticeable. The Bible tells us that King Herod had to ask the Magi where it was. Although astronomers have searched through the ages for any hint of a star, or comet, or whatever, which would support the Bible story, nothing that high in the sky could have marked out a country let alone a stable. Such a search was like looking for the end of the rainbow. There is another simple explanation – as on any clear night we can all see the lights of aircraft, so much like very bright stars, moving slowly across the sky and low enough to be followed.

And what about the actions of the Magi themselves, better known to most of us as the three wise men? Was it their wisdom which agreed to a secret meeting with the local King Herod to tell him they were looking for the new King of the Jews who was to be born in Herod's kingdom. And was it wise to tell him all about the star which was guiding them? They also agreed, once they had found the new baby, that they would return to let Herod know where the child lay, and were only stopped by a warning given in a dream. The consequences of their actions and their failure to return caused Herod to give the order to kill all the baby boys in Bethlehem and its vicinity who were two years old or under. What a terrible price God extracted from the innocents. Why?

Meanwhile the angels, who must have known something that the wise men did not, had foreseen that Herod would kill Jesus for they warned the Magi not to go back. They were also aware of the consequences of their action because, once more in a dream, they commanded Joseph to take the child and his mother to Egypt. Does it strike you, as it does me, that it's a strange sort of all powerful God who, as a direct result of spreading the word of the birth of Christ through his angels and his star, caused many innocent babies to be killed. He seemed able to deal with Zechariah and Joseph but not Herod. Why? Calming Herod by visiting him in his sleep or by threatening him should, according to what is recorded in the Bible, have been quite normal for the angels. Matthew's gospel says that following Herod's death the angel again appeared in Joseph's dream to say there was now no danger and he should return the child and his mother to Israel. It is difficult to believe that those mothers and fathers who had had their babies killed would have had any sympathy with Christ had they known this. What would you have done in similar circumstances? I cannot accept that an all-seeing God handled the situation so ineptly.

In the end both families, who were highly favoured by God,

28

were used to give life to John the Baptist and Jesus Christ and to bring them up as their own children, and they lived to see them die terrible deaths by the hand of Man. Why were they not better protected by the God whose children they really were? Where were the angels when they were needed or were they only able to make appearances and offer explanations? Certainly those people to whom they spoke, like Mary and Joseph, Elizabeth and Zechariah, the wise men and the shepherds, had all been convinced enough to obey their commands. Why not some of the 'baddies' of the Bible?

Looking more closely at the life of Jesus the gospels clearly show that he had some extraordinary powers for the times in which he lived as well as being an extremely effective orator. But if he had arrived with those same powers today, as Man's world approaches the Twenty First Century, how would his miracles be seen? The world of the 1990s is dripping with scepticism and, despite the fact that we remain gullible, there is an underlying strong belief that no-one does anything for nothing. For those millions of us with televisions we are better informed, sometimes even manipulated in our thinking, and are entertained by magicians who are so brilliant that impossible acts are regularly performed, each one, almost of necessity, outshining the last. Yet although we cannot see how it is done we know it is all clever illusions using specially designed equipment and sleight of hand, and we admire the performers. Nevertheless it still seems impossible. A few hundred years ago performers of similar acts were branded sorcerers or witches and burnt at the stake in the belief that the devil had been conjured up to help.

So how would today's sceptic world react to Christ and many of his miracles if he turned up again? Would anyone really believe what they read or were told, or even what they saw? They would even doubt the stories told by friends who had been personally involved, being sure that they had misunderstood what they had witnessed. Man's conditioned thinking, his growing distrust of his own kind, and his limited knowledge of strange phenomenon would not allow him to accept anything which would cause him discomfort, however minor. Most people would cross to the other side of the street to avoid getting involved. It is more interesting to consider what we would do if we really did believe that we could get something for nothing without any obligation to the giver.

Jesus's life, as recorded in the gospels, was a strange mixture of parables, unusual behaviour and miracles. Many of his miracles were in curing the sick, a remarkable number of them being, according to the gospels, possessed by demons, an expression that no longer exists in medical circles though many of today's sadistically cruel killers could fall into that category. The dead were brought back to life, although Jesus himself said when asked to help with Jairus's daughter that the girl was not dead but asleep. On that occasion he permitted only three of his followers and the child's father and mother to enter the house where the child lay. He had arrived late because someone in the jostling crowd had healed themselves by touching the hem of his garment, and Mark records, at once Jesus realized as the power had gone out from him, a remark which stimulates thought. In the Jairus miracle, as in many others, Jesus gave strict orders not to let anyone know about it. Why? There was a crowd outside Jairus's house who must have heard the announcement that his daughter was dead and who later saw her alive and indeed they had laughed at Jesus when he said she was only asleep. That seems to me to suggest that what Jesus instructed them to be quiet about was what had happened inside the house. It was not unusual for Jesus to instruct the recipient of his miracles to tell no-one but since he was followed on many occasions by a multitude who would have witnessed the result it does seem an extraordinary comment to make unless he was trying to create an image of mystery. Think about it.

The remarkable advances we have seen in recent years in medical science has brought cures to many illnesses. In some parts of the world which are still being decimated by those illnesses miracles are being performed on the poor sojourners. Fifty years ago these cures would have been classed as miracles anywhere on earth. And bringing back people to life has become an everyday occurrence in many parts of the world by using new drugs, equipment or techniques, perhaps the best known method in the latter category is the kiss of life, although for many years before that drowned or electrocuted people were brought back to life with other resuscitation methods. How would such modern techniques have looked to our forefathers in the Victorian era, only one hundred years ago?

30

How would they have been seen in the Middle Ages?

To a world with today's knowledge some of Jesus's miracles could be seen as relatively ordinary but it is important to remember that they were performed some two thousand years ago. But we can now see that the miracles could have arisen from the knowledge well in advance of Jesus's time rather than the holy magic of God.

But the resurrection on which the whole faith of Christianity is founded needs much deeper thought for if it took place as recorded in the Bible it cannot be equalled in today's terms. Also there, in the New Testament, is the story of Lazarus whose return to life was even more impressive than that of Jesus. That story tells how Martha and Mary, who Jesus loved, sought his help when Mary's brother Lazarus was dying. However Jesus stayed where he was for two more days so that by the time he arrived at Martha and Mary's village Lazarus was dead. It is this story that records the smallest sentence in the Bible – Jesus wept. However he went to the tomb, which, like his own, was a cave with a stone laid across the entrance, and Martha warned him about the nasty smell since Lazarus had lain there for four days. He asked them to roll away the stone and called out in a loud voice for Lazarus to come out, which he did still wrapped with strips of linen and a cloth about his face. One is left with the impression from the comments about the smell that Lazarus's body had rotted, in which case here was a miracle indeed.

But Jesus's action of ignoring the cri de coeur for two days must be familiar to many people as a human failing. The result was that he inflicted a great deal of pain on the friends he loved for no apparent purpose. With all his Godly power could he not foresee that? The Bible does not tell what kept him where he was which prompts the question, was it not recorded because it was unimportant? Why then did he not go to Martha and Mary?

At another time, says Mark, John complained to Jesus that some stranger was driving out demons using his name and the disciple had told him to stop.

'Do not stop him,' Jesus said. 'No one who does a miracle in my name can in the next moment say anything bad about me, for whoever is not against us is for us.'

Now, to me, while I understand the philosophy I cannot help but wonder who were these unnamed people who were able to perform miracles at the same time as Jesus? Doesn't it make you wonder?

Jesus flatly refused to give any signs which would prove he was who he claimed to be. Surely he could have got his important message across much more convincingly had he allowed the way he performed his miracles to be seen or had provided some global sign which his opponents wanted. The latter would have set back his critics and proved himself to those who remained unsure. Would God, creator of the universe, have hesitated to show his awesome power? Would he not have produced a world-wide sign if he wanted everyone on the planet to know that he was the one and only God whose laws must be obeyed?

The basis of the teachings of Christianity are founded on the writings of the gospels which were interpreted by the learned churchmen of the time. Those teachings, which some found difficult to accept or understand, demanded unquestioning faith. Christians' thoughts have been conditioned over many centuries to accept that premise and any ideas which arose which did not meet the faith's stated beliefs were dealt with quickly and firmly. Today there are many differing Christian religious denominations founded on his teachings and, although the day to day practices of worship vary considerably, the basic precept that Jesus Christ was the son of God is taught by all. Each denomination also claims the Bible as the authority for its teachings. The question which must arise is, that if some of the interpretations can differ in this way, are the interpretations of the basic scriptures which all denominations are taught, both Old and New Testament, correct?

The need for the writings to be studied again in the light of Man's knowledge today is clear. We must look questioningly not only at what the scriptures actually say but at the gaps where nothing is said at all. We must search for any signs which show that Jesus was not simply a man with knowledge well in advance of the rest of those on earth with an able back-up team. The other side of the coin must also be studied by modern Man to see how human Jesus was in the things that he did and the way that he did them. It means setting aside the interpretations which have been cemented into the minds of all people by conditioned thinking over many centuries.

For on this planet Man is a newcomer. For the first time in

his short history there is a small but growing awareness that the future of his planet, and indeed of his heirs, cannot be left to the God about which he has been taught. He is slowly beginning to realize that it is only Man himself who can deal with the problems of his world. He can now see his world as an insignificant speck in a universe he knows little about. In power and knowledge he is aware that he is but a new born infant. He can see the gaping chasm which separates the power, magnificence and ordered symmetry of the universe from the religious teachings of any faith on earth. He is aware that nature controls the universe and his stumbling actions, long lauded as achievements of Man, can bring naturally occurring disasters. Yet he knows of no other intelligent being.

All this leads me to only one conclusion and that is, as far as Man on earth is concerned, there is God and there is god.

3

It is a sad reflection of our small world that there are so many people who are unaware of its wonders or those which surround it. Amongst those fortunate enough to be able to read there can be no doubt that there is some massive form of incredible power which not only created the billions of stars, planets, comets and other bodies all hurtling through space at tremendous speeds, but one which extends through billions and billions of miles controlling temperatures, speeds, and indeed the relationships of the whole of the universe.

Planet earth itself is just an extremely minute part of one galaxy which is made up of millions of stars, and that galaxy itself is just one of the millions of galaxies which are distributed through the visible universe. All the stars and galaxies are in constant motion, many of them with enormous velocities which, because of the astronomical distances they are from earth, can only be perceived by using delicate instruments.

The earth gets most of its chemical energy from the sun which has a surface temperature of some five thousand seven hundred degrees centigrade reaching over one million degrees just beneath its surface. Although these temperatures are themselves astronomical it is fascinating to note that the earth's core is hotter than the surface of the sun. The sun can release massive nuclear energy which is transmitted by radiation and convection to its outer layers and then to space, a very small part of which reaches earth. Life on earth, both animal and plant, is dependent upon the bombardment of the rays of the sun which, were it not for the protection of earth's atmosphere, could become lethal. I always wonder what we are bombarded with from the earth's core as there must be nuclear activity there too.

The velocity of earth at a given point at the equator exceeds a thousand miles per hour, whilst the velocity in its orbit round the sun is some sixty-six thousand miles an hour. What awesome power is it that moves it at these speeds and has done so for millions of years without any visible means of propulsion. Is there a simple explanation that we can all understand?

I personally think it impossible, except perhaps for those closely involved with astronomy, to appreciate even the distances involved in the solar system let alone the universe itself. The sun is about ninety-three million miles away from earth with the next nearest star being some two hundred and fifty thousand times that distance. And yet, although by terrestrial standards the solar system occupies a large volume of space, it is only a very tiny fraction of the whole universe. Limitless space. Man can only marvel at the immensity of the power that holds the solar system together, with the moon circling earth attracting its waters, producing the tides, while the earth plus eight other planets, all orbit the sun in their individual timescales and paths. Comets too pass earth from time to time on their predetermined routes and it seems quite possible to me that there are some, of which Man is yet unaware, whose regular and unchanging journey takes many thousands of years before returning into earth's range of vision again. Man has to admit his knowledge of what is happening in space is extremely limited.

Even within the solar system there are many little understood phenomena such as the Van Allen radiation belts which are two layers of radiation trapped in the outer atmosphere by earth's magnetic field. There are also minor planets of the solar system which lie in a belt between Mars and Jupiter. The belt contains thousands of millions of particles, from dust to some one thousand six hundred recognized larger asteroids or planetoids, the largest of which is Ceres which is said to be over four hundred miles in diameter. From time to time gravitational forces push the asteroids out of the belt into a new orbit which, unlike the major planets, can cross earth's own orbit and collide with it.

There is evidence on earth's land of many collisions with asteroids whilst many others, as yet undetected, will have fallen into the oceans. I can understand the theory that a collision with an asteroid as large as Ceres would cause, at least, a massive movement of earth or water into the atmosphere blocking out the warmth and light of the sun. I also understand the results could prevent photosynthesis so necessary to life which would prove fatal to billions of living things. Many scientists believe that it was such a phenomenon that brought about the extinction of the dinosaurs which had ruled the world for over one hundred and forty million years. But long before we arrived here. It's fascinating! As it is to think of all heavenly bodies suspended in mid air with no visible means of support, held in place by some force we barely understand and over which we have no control whatsoever. Even in our own time there have been some near misses by large bodies hurtling through space which would have brought global problems had they struck but none of them were anywhere near the size of Ceres.

Man's knowledge even of his own planet is still in its infancy. Some three quarters of it is covered by water which remains largely unexplored and Man is just discovering that life exists under massive pressures in the deepest oceans of the world. Whilst it is general knowledge that Mount Everest is the highest land mountain in the world, few are aware where the deepest ocean lies. Even today there is doubt about the existence of any as yet undiscovered large creatures which may be living in the waters of the world.

The distance from the bed of the deepest ocean depth to the highest land peak is over twelve miles, a relatively tiny distance. And on this small planet above sea level lies a land mass which displays scenery of indescribable beauty, of rugged splendour, of inhospitable deserts of intense heat and equally inhospitable frozen wastes. Even Man's estimates of the age of the earth vary in magnitude from several hundred million to one and a half billion years. Many secrets of the past must lie covered by the changes over that time. Great gusting convulsive volcanic eruptions giving birth to new lands or destroying others, lands eroded by time and weather, drowning beneath the seas. The Antarctic continent covering an area larger than Europe (including European Russia) and measuring nearly ten per cent of the earth's total landmass, is nearly entirely covered with sheet ice. What history lies in the land beneath? And have the poles always been where they are today?

In many parts of his world Man is surrounded by the beauty of nature all in a bright colourful pageant. Even the space surrounding his world has a kaleidoscopical picture changing from the light blue of dawn, through the deep blue of day to the glowing red of sunset, often sprinkled with white cotton wool-like clouds skudding across it. At night a black backcloth sets off the twinkling jewel-like stars in an every day scene which Man scarcely notices.

The animal world too has its local fascination of rabbits, squirrels, hedgehogs, frogs and thousands of other small creatures, while the world's regions have a wealth of large animals some of which are said to be virtually the same as they were millions of years ago. It makes you wonder why animals of that length of existence do not have a higher intelligence than newly arrived Man. Earth is also freely populated by a myriad of beautiful multi-coloured wild birds. And even today Man is only just discovering new creatures which inhabit the earth in which he is king. He continues, generally in a jocular way, to search for those legendary large animals such as the Loch Ness monster, Bigfoot and the Yeti, each leaving a number of tangible signs which cannot easily be explained away.

But he has very little control over his small world and is vulnerable to the whims of nature. He is unable to forecast the outbreaks of violence which erupt from the bowels of the earth, shaking loose the Man-made structures and devastating whole communities. He can love or hate the sun, depending on whether he faces it as warm and life-giving in one country or the relentless reaper of death in another. He has no control over the rain, so fickle in its decisions of where and when it will fall, sometimes simply a nuisance borne grudgingly, at other times creating havoc in heavy downfalls. Too often it causes death on a massive scale simply by failing to appear when it is needed.

And it is the same power that holds the white fluffy clouds of summer together herding them across the sky. And the warm and cold fronts provided by nature, which bring bands of cloud large enough to shield whole countries from the heat of the sun by day or the frost by night, can also bring violent electrical storms, torrential rain, hail and snow. The world is full of wonder sometimes not visible to Man's naked eye, such as the beauty of the individual and exquisitely designed snowflakes produced by some unseen hand guided by a power that appreciates symmetry. While the seasons on the planet bring changes to its scenery, like some giant artist spreading his individual cloaks of colour over thousands of miles of land and seascapes for just a few short weeks. And accompanying those seasonal changes comes the increase or decrease in temperature which affects the lives of every living thing on earth.

The animal inhabitants have had to adapt to the changes in order to survive. As they detect the oncoming changes from the warmth of summer to the cold of winter, or vice versa, the great migration or hibernation takes place all over the globe. With the freedom of the skies the birds can travel thousands of miles each year across oceans which have no landmarks apparent to Man, and are able to return with unerring accuracy not only to the country of their birth but indeed to the same nests. Fish too cover great distances through the oceans of the world returning to spawn in the same rivers in which they were born. I read with fascination that all fresh water eels are born in the Sargasso Sea and each year eels from the rivers of the world swim back to their birthplace to spawn. The Sargasso Sea itself is an interesting area of still water at the centre of ocean currents in the North Atlantic Ocean and is identified by the floating island-like mass of seaweed which covers its area. The inbuilt guidance system of all animals, their ability to scent danger or track their objectives, are gifts far greater than those of Man.

Man's daily environment is established by the weather and in recent years satellites have been introduced to try to improve his ability to predict it. But even for short periods ahead, as the weather can vary so much from locale to locale, his forecasts can only serve as a guide. Long range forecasts are simply an informed guess with no credibility. Man's inability even in the short term to predict the weather shows up all too clearly when so many of his attempts to conquer the more inhospitable regions of the world have failed because of an unexpected deterioration in the unpredictable weather. Films of expeditions undertaken over recent years show this very dramatically and many brave people have died through the whims of the weather.

The monsoon regions of Asia have three months of almost non-stop torrential rain each year and local farmers have to gamble, often with their lives, on the right time to plant their crops. If the rains arrive a few days too early the crops are washed from the ground, a few days too late and the crops have died. Without the ability to predict the arrival date of the rainy seasons they select a mid point for the norm and that usually works. What force brings them round at almost the same time each year to stay for their prescribed period before disappearing to who knows where for another year?

The late, or non-arrival of the rains brings drought and death. The Bible itself mentions the droughts and famines in East Africa and history records they have continued unabated ever since with disastrous loss of life. The 1980s has produced one famine following another with millions of people dying of starvation due to the failure of the crops from lack of water. So, even after many years of research Man is unable to forecast, or to deal with, such major catastrophes. Is it the lack of will to help those unable to help themselves?

The great irony is that although Man has no knowledge on how to control the weather his actions on earth are inadvertently affecting it. Scientists throughout the world are raising their voices in a developing clamour for action to be taken to stop those activities on earth which, should nothing be done, will bring adverse effects to all inhabitants of the planet.

One such concern arises from the knowledge that, over the last thirty to forty years small increases in global temperatures have taken place, more in the last ten to fifteen years. The so-called 'greenhouse effect' is said to be due to high levels of carbon dioxide in the earth's atmosphere brought about partly by Man's use of fossil fuels over the last hundred to two hundred years, partly by large increases in the use of charcoal and also by the rapidly growing number of cars pushing out the gas from their exhausts. The carbon dioxide layer thus formed around the globe lets heat into the earth's atmosphere but not out thus acting like glass in a greenhouse.

The weather pattern of the 1980s across the world has produced an abnormal number of freak climatic conditions which has served to highlight the concern expressed by the scientific community. There are signs that some governments are at last paying attention to the warnings but it is a world problem which can only be tackled by all governments together. Their slowness to respond, or in many cases their inactivity, indicates to their people a lack of concern which is lulling them trustingly into a feeling of languor. Because, like so many other things in life, it requires specialist knowledge individuals have to rely on the advice of the scientists and the governments which they serve. Yet it seems the former is calling for actions to reduce the amounts of carbon dioxide being dispersed in the air while the latter seem impervious to such pleas. But public concern is growing and has brought a new Green Party to politics which had made other parties begin to react at last. It will take time to halt the increase, let alone start a decrease, but there is enough evidence even to the undiscerning to indicate that the problem must be tackled now.

Unhindered by these activities the winds, currents, volcanic eruptions, hot springs, rivers in the sea like the Gulf Stream, and all the natural growth encouraged by the sun, all operate without the aid or, often, even the understanding of Man. We have no idea who or what created the senses by which we, and the other animals of this planet, are aware of our environment or recognize changes in our own bodily conditions, such as pain, movement of muscles and joints, or cold and warmth. The five senses of sight, hearing, smell, taste, and touch, which provide all animals with knowledge of their external world, are gifts from some unknown but powerful source. And what causes the incredible feeling of true love like that of a mother or father who would unquestioningly sacrifice their own life to save those of their children? When such love passes between a man and a woman the glow of happiness, sheer delight and pleasure each feels for the other is indescribable. Such gifts are priceless.

It doesn't matter what you call it, there exists an awesome power far beyond our understanding and, regardless of how we may try to unlock the secrets of that power, the key question keeps recurring about who or what created it? This super-power is the creator, not just of every grain of sand of our very minute world, of our every feeling of love, hate, pleasure, pain but is also the creator of the whole massive universe of which Man is an infinitesimal and negligible part. Whichever of the seemingly endless religions Man embraces this power must be, by whatever name is chosen, the true God.

By comparison to that massive power the abilities of the God of the Bible are insignificant and he shrinks to the status of chief of a tribe on a tiny planet. Look at how the Bible sets out in the first five books of the Old Testament, the books of Moses, God's instructions to Man. It records there that God spoke regularly to Moses setting out the laws that he wanted obeyed. Failure to follow those instructions was met with swift and unrelenting punishment and often involving killing whole communities. The only option offered by the God of the Bible was to follow his laws or accept the consequences, really no option at all. The God of the Bible gave Moses a covenant for him to pass to his people for their acceptance. They, being aware of the consequences of not accepting it, did so.

The use of aggressive threats by the powerful to achieve their objectives has long been the rule of Man but there is a major difference between the objectives of the Bible's God and Man. The former was threatening punishment for behaviour which would harm the future of the human race, the latter has created fear by evil so that a few can control millions.

It is the Book of Exodus which sets out the ten commandments of God which formed the basis from which Man has reinterpreted his own meanings and his own laws. Few people today could recite all ten commandments, or even broadly give God's detailed instructions, as set out in the following three chapters of Exodus, on how these commandments should be applied. One of the great problems in quoting from the Bible itself is that, to many, it is a book of contradiction and can be used to argue diametrically opposed views. We therefore need to think more about the basic beliefs which we were taught rather than argue too closely on interpretations.

Whether we realize it or not, Man's formative years while rising to adulthood are essentially full of advice, guidance and coercion towards conditioning his or her thinking. The first five years of life for children are spent with parents spelling out their rules, learning to avoid danger and establishing themselves socially. For the next fifteen or so years at schools, colleges and universities he or she is presented with facts and interpretations, the former being based on the latest discoveries in science, medicine, etc., and the latter on fashions or changes in customs or practice. He or she is also taught religion. Their success during the latter years is measured by testing how well they have learned what they have been taught and often calls for a good memory recall rather than original thought. Religious knowledge studies use interpretations of the Bible which have changed little over many generations.

41

Since the commandments form the basis of our early laws we have to look more closely at Exodus. There the seventh commandment which we all know clearly says, Thou shalt not kill, but the covenant defines certain circumstances where God set the penalty of death to be administered for a number of crimes. These included:

Death for a premeditated killing.

Death for striking father or mother.

Death for stealing and selling a man.

Death for cursing father or mother.

Death for hurting a woman with child which results in death.

Death to the owners of oxen who knew their beast to be likely to gore someone and he let it wander loose.

Death by the sword for afflicting any widow, or fatherless child, and,

'Thou shalt not suffer a witch to live.

Whosoever lieth with a beast shall surely be put to death.

He that sacrificieth unto any god, save unto the Lord only, he shall be utterly destroyed.' And,

'No blood is shed for a thief killed in the act.'

The covenant also covered a wide range of other laws some of which exist in similar forms today. An example could be:

'And thou shalt take no gift: for the gift bindeth the wise, and perverteth the words of the righteous.'

Do these laws not seem to you like those of a head of government? And can you see how Man has carefully filtered out those laws he does not want? If they were truly the words of God the Creator could Man set himself up to be greater than God? For that is what he is doing when he changes those laws. Even humane acts like abandoning the death penalty could be seen as overruling God.

But Exodus goes further, for in addition to the laws and punishments that God set out, which are assumed to have been given for the whole human race to follow, the covenant deals with very local matters. Thus God promised Moses that the angels would overthrow his people's enemies, and even mentions who they are, fellow humans but of a different tribe! On this Exodus says:

'By little and little I will drive them out from before thee, until thou be increased and inherit the land.

'And I will set thy bounds from the Red Sea even unto the sea of the Philistines, and from the desert unto the river: for I will deliver the inhabitants of the land into your hand; and thou shalt drive them out before thee.

'Thou shalt make no covenant with them, nor with their Gods. They shall not dwell in thy land, lest they make thee sin against me: for if thou serve their Gods, it will surely be a snare unto thee.'

Such local instructions are entirely consistent with the way Man acts but surely totally inconsistent with any true God dealing with his creation? The Bible's God seemed to be fighting for power in the way many other world leaders have over the centuries.

Throughout the books 'the Lord spake unto Moses' and seemed to take particular care that others were kept at a distance, although they were encouraged to approach near enough to see some of the lighting and other effects that he was able to produce. Others were treated to spectacles like thunder and lightning, the noise of a trumpet and the mountain smoking. Would a God really present such theatrical stunts? Even with the very important tables of stone with the commandments Moses was told to go up to the mount alone and he disappeared from the watching elders into a cloud, thus hiding God from them. We are taught that God is all around us, invisibly watching our actions, why then was it so necessary for the God of the Bible to use clouds to hide and warn Moses of dire consequences to anyone who saw him? I remember very similar tactics were used by the great Wizard of Oz!

We can only assume that Moses was with God collecting the tables for some time for by the time he had returned to the people they had melted down their gold into the figure of a calf. When they began worshipping their creation, contrary to the covenant they had just accepted, God was not happy and was all for consuming them there and then, but Moses talked them round. They did not go unpunished as the sons of Levi had to take their swords and go in and out of every gate throughout the camp and slay every man and his brother, and every man and his companion, and every man and his neighbour. This, says the Old Testament, the children of Levi did, slaying about three thousand men. How can this God, who seems to have so many of the frailties apparent in Man, be compared in any way to the giver of all life and creator of the universe? No, somewhere along the way Man has mixed his Gods.

So where would that leave those claiming to be God's earthly representatives, of which there were many, one of them being Christ? Were they representing God or a god? These differing representatives do seem responsible for dividing this small world into the religious factions we have today, all claiming theirs is the true God. We can all see that they have been the cause of wars for centuries, and still today are used to justify many abhorrent atrocities heaped by Man upon his fellows. All these representatives of God have threatened the human race with penalties if they do not mend their ways. Are these threats real or just window dressing for those of inferior intelligence? There is absolutely no doubt that the power which created and holds the universe together is one power. The living creatures on earth, except for Man, all follow the rules of nature, i.e. one power. Would such a single all-powerful force send what appears to be differing and, since they had failed to bring love and peace to the world, such inadequate representatives. The creator of the universe clearly has the power to demonstrate, without any doubt at all, that he is the one and only God. Those who use the argument of faith have closed their minds, which must be opened, for failure to do so will affect their future and maybe even destroy it.

What is it in us that causes us to think that we are apart from the rest of the animal kingdom, and that God's representatives have only come to save him and not the creator's planet and all its life? After all, despite the opening paragraphs of the Bible, we have now accepted that the animals inhabited this world millions of years before Man's arrival. It is more their world than ours.

Looking at that very short history and the state of the world today can it be said that Man's time on earth has been anything but a disaster? That is not only for Man himself but for all other creatures of the world, or don't they matter? To Man life is cheap, whether those of his own race prematurely taken in the thousands of wars and battles so lauded in history but which in reality have ripped mankind apart, or those of earth's animals which have been destroyed in their billions. Man's other activities are causing pollution to his planet and are becoming life threatening for all forms of life on earth. Gases put into the air have affected the atmosphere of the planet and brought acid rain which is devastating plant life in some parts of the world. Pollution created by the wide use of fertilizers and pesticides which get washed by the rain into the rivers and thus into the seas are being blamed for contributing to the deaths of many plants and creatures living in the oceans. In this century rabbits, considered by Man to be a scourge, were almost wiped out by the disease mixamatosis and, although they recovered, Man still uses the painful and distressing disease to control the rabbit population.

Each year the world watches as young seals are clubbed to death to cull the population. And there was the additional tragedy of thousands of seals being washed up on the shores of the countries of the North Sea to die a terrible death with many scientists blaming pollution for their lack of resistance to the killer virus. No-one knows the reality of what is happening in the oceans caused by pollution. No-one knows how much waste is really being put into the sea. There are many cases brought to the courts of illegal dumping of toxic wastes on land because, sooner or later, they are discovered. Not so in the sea. No-one knows, does anyone care?

Lives of plants have no significance whatsoever in Man's plan of life unless they are useful to him. He has committed rape on land and in the sea in his endeavours either to enrich his own existence or merely to demonstrate, often to himself in order to boost his own ego, his superiority over all other forms of life.

Does Man really believe that the superpower, the God, would give him this planet to use or abuse as he thinks fit with scant regard for the older inhabitants and plant life which have taken literally millions of years to develop. Sadly, such is the arrogance of Man, some people do. But that may be because the God they have been taught to believe in is as human as they are.

As a race Man must begin to gather the strings of the massive but unco-ordinated world organizations and nurture them towards a single objective, the future of Mankind. While the present situation remains, where national interests remain the dominant priority, leaders will continue to extract as much wealth as possible from those parts of the world which they control, sometimes by fear, sometimes by consent. How much longer can individuals representing the great majority of earth's inhabitants claim that they can but watch helplessly at the death and destruction which others are heaping upon their world in order to achieve their individual or collective objectives? How much longer can you and I blame it on them? They only represent us while we allow them to. The problem is that too many of those in power seem to need it as a drug and, like all addicts, do not care what methods, or pain, or deceit, are used to obtain and then hold it.

But at last in the differing nations of the world the murmurings of the protesting few are growing into a new rumbling awareness amongst the masses of the dreadful harm Man has been inflicting on his world. Unfortunately very few protests are rising about the pain and anguish that is being inflicted on their fellow men. Sadly too, many protestors have made a hobby or lifestyle of protesting simply to advance their political aims or their own personal status. Such selfish actions have detracted from those genuinely concerned for the future of the world and have thus braked progress. The health of the planet is inextricably linked to what is happening to the world's human population and one cannot be dealt with without the other.

All over the world Man has lost his ability to be honest with his fellows or indeed with himself. Facts are twisted and presented in differing ways by those in positions of trust in order to forward their own cause regardless of the worry it brings to vulnerable people, as they succeed only in confusing those who need to know the truth. In some societies only one view is allowed, thus quashing all dissention. In either case acceptance or otherwise of interpretations of facts depends to a great extent on individual's conditioned thinking, for that is the way he has been taught to think. Faced with conflicting opinions, disagreements on what the facts say, and fiery oratory, individuals find they are unable to make informed judgements and thus revert to the conditioned thinking stage. Man is generally a gregarious animal and needs to conform to feel comfortable.

In almost every field today there is a strong rivalry amongst the world's experts who, again, wishing to advance their own view and status, air their disagreements in public. This only succeeds in bringing greater fear and confusion to those who rely on their informed advice being sound, sometimes in life or death situations. Collaboration to help the people of the world who desperately need help often becomes a game of national importance. Attitudes are drawn based upon some hierarchical system which the individual, or the nation, has put into its conditioned thinking. The word rival itself is defined in the dictionary as 'a person's competitor for some prize'. The prize Mankind needs is the future of the world, not the aspirations of individuals or even groups or nations.

Many, many things which Man does could be seen as a throwback to his origins. There are strongly held views that Man's future is mapped out before him. Shakespeare's Hamlet put it well when he said:

'There's a divinity that shapes our ends,
Rough-hew them how we will.'

Man's origin and ultimate survival can be said to be laid out in the Bible but the interpretations which we are taught are getting us deeper into anarchy. We need to look at the message, for from it we can see many of the political ideas of Man, including the extremes of fascism and communism. We can see too the answer to the question of immortality. Many of today's problems of the growing violence throughout the world is due to civilized thinkers preaching that Man's inhumanity to Man must not be procreated. This thought from the past taken out of context is a dangerous path to follow.

Do you ever wonder why many of us are so concerned about our pasts? Why we are forever digging things up and fighting to prevent others being taken down. Why are we so concerned about the future of the world after our death? Is re-incarnation a myth or fact? Do ghosts exist? And, uncomfortably, the fundamental question which keeps us hanging on to the religious teachings, almost afraid to know the truth; is there life after death? These, and other similar questions, need answers which we have to understand if we are to calm our nagging minds. Blind faith is no longer enough, for it asks us not to question what our fellows are telling us. Where do they get the monopoly on life's meaning? Who taught them? When an

47

important leader voices his doubts, such as those of David Jenkins, the Bishop of Durham, he is criticized because his critics claim that doubts expressed by such an august member of the church shakes the faith of others. Surely such a dogmatic approach to God cannot be right; indeed is it not such an attitude that has caused so much intolerance, bigotry and hatred in our world? Take time to look at your beliefs and question them, setting aside all the conditioned thinking which has remained in your minds throughout your life. It will not be easy, for some it may be impossible, but a recognition that there are such thoughts will help.

Consider what you have been taught about Man's past. Look particularly at whether, and how, your thoughts could change if you accepted that God the Creator was the scientific process which produced the universe, stars, planets, gravity, and atmosphere, all down to the minutest particle, with life evolving over millions of years. Plant life, animal life, intelligent life. And then consider a separate God, the God of the Bible. Assume, for the moment, that he and his angels had evolved from the scientific process but not on this planet, but he came here and became the creator of Man. Don't reject the theory before looking at the way our race is behaving and see the possibility that we could shortly find ourselves in a similar position with, in perhaps a century or so, the knowledge to do something about it. How many of us, given the chance, would flee this world to another as beautiful as this one where we would be the only intelligent being on the planet and thus the King, or God? What rules would you introduce to prevent the horrors which you are leaving behind repeating themselves?

Now look again at the scriptures and our world.

4

It is Ecclesiastes that says:
and there is no new thing under the sun.

When, in the middle of the nineteenth century, Darwin propounded his theories on Man's ancestry and the principle of natural selection they were bitterly contested by contemporaries on theological grounds. While they were fully acceptable for animals, the theories stuck in the throat as far as Mankind was concerned as they were against basic religious teachings.

But history is punctuated with people who had the temerity to question established teachings. Over four hundred years ago, throughout the world, the church and state view that human beings and their planet were the centre of God's province was challenged by Nicolaus Copernicus who had the effrontery to suggest that the earth was only one of several planets revolving round a fairly small star. In the early part of the seventeenth century his findings got the support of Kepler and Galileo. All of them suffered as church and state roundly condemned them as heretics. Although Galileo was forced by the church to renounce his findings the seeds of doubt had been sown and the erosion of the hitherto inflexible view of churchmen had begun.

Nineteenth century society too was shocked to the roots at Darwin's theories and he too experienced the wrath of church and establishment. Even the thought that Man could supposedly be related to the common creatures of the world was unthinkable and rather de trop. However, as science progressed, Darwin's theories achieved credibility and it was not long before eminent people began to search for the missing link between Man and apes. Today many major museums display drawings which indicate how Man may have evolved. The genetic similarity between Man and apes seemed to confirm the relationship but the direct link has not yet been established.

49

It is possible that the difficulty Man has had in finding his origins are that he has restricted his thinking and research to his own planet. The development of most animals over millions of years can be rationalized by comparing one with another, and although their shape and form has changed to suit their environments and life-styles they do not have the ability to think as Man does. The theory of Man evolving from apes still rests uneasily in the minds of many, raising such questions about why apes themselves, or indeed other animals whose species have existed for many millions of years, have not developed the power of rational thought.

Would our past teachings and scientific theories become more meaningful if it were assumed Man arrived on earth from another planet altogether and used the apes to establish himself here? Today more than ever before, with the advantages of greater knowledge and the ability to express views without the fear of castigation, with freer thinking and with a growing despair about where the world is going, this possibility must be seriously considered.

Wherever Man looks for his origins there is an inevitable return to the fundamental question of why he is here at all. With his ability to think he has long considered that there must be more to life than the prayer book's three score years and ten, such a tiny drop in the vast oceans of time. Certainly by the beginning of the twenty second century virtually every one of those alive on earth today, about five thousand million people, will be long dead and buried, as will many more thousands of millions as yet to be born. Even if medical science were to bring a significant increase in life expectancy, death of a body is inevitable which still leaves unanswered the perennial question which arises with each generation; is there life after death?

All animals, including Man, fear death. Only Man has the disability of being able to hide his emotions and pretend that there is no fear. In the male of the human species this attitude is encouraged by conditioned thinking which teaches that only weaklings show fear. But that does not mean that fear is not felt. And often, because society is always ready to condemn those it thinks are weak, individuals have to hide it by using drugs or alcohol. When death touches, everyone feels, amongst the pain and anguish, the fear of death itself.

It is those who are left behind who can sometimes see death

as a blessed relief either because a loved one has, in their eyes, suffered enough, or because of the pain they themselves have had to endure watching the wicked process of death. Often, in order to close the great gaping chasm left in their lives when a loved one dies, people have a need to cling to something, or someone, as a life-raft through the turbulent time ahead. Within themselves, and those trying to comfort them, lie the teachings of the church which states that the family will meet again in heaven. The vision of everlasting damnation in hell, also advanced in the teachings of the church, has long since lost its credibility and use, except perhaps to satisfy hatred.

But still, after hundreds, maybe thousands of years of thought and heart searching, the human race is no nearer knowing whether there is life after death or not. There is a general acceptance that there is no after-life for the rest of the world's animals but Man's egocentric view cannot accept that it applies to him. He wants a reason for his life and needs to believe there is something more. But with that belief should be a driving need for Man to live in peace with all members of his own race as well as for protecting the assets of his world against abuse. A hundred years ago the people of developed nations had trust in their rulers to work together to protect them and to see that justice was evenly applied throughout the world against those who would harm them. As Mankind prepares for the next century, injustice and terror occurs every day and goes unpunished, indeed encouraged, in many areas of the world. Throughout every nation the people's trust has been eroded by leaders abusing it too often. This has resulted in people not only questioning what is, or is not, being done in their name but it has also caused them to doubt whether they are being told the truth.

This doubt has added to those about religious teachings brought on by advances in scientific knowledge. Religious hatred and bigotry has fuelled the fires of confusion and raised further unanswerable questions. And yet most people still believe in God but feel that religious portrayals of him today no longer represent their image of him. For while they see their God as kind, loving and forgiving, the religious factions are using his name to support indescribable horrors on their fellow Man. Such fanaticism still calls for blind faith in the beliefs of the church which for the majority of normal people is no longer

51

enough. The question is being asked whether the world is clinging to the belief in immortality in the desperate hope that it is true, for without it the reason for life becomes more obscure. But can people still relate to the picture drawn by the churches of the spirit leaving the body at death and entering the gates of heaven? Man's comprehension cannot picture what form such a spirit would retain, for without the same features of the body how could recognition be made? Indeed, for that to happen anyway, memories of life on earth would have to be retained and many would not wish to do so.

Human beings have a strange regard for dead bodies, questioning the ethics of so many surgeons who want to use parts of these bodies to enhance the lives of the living. There is even some fear or moral stupidity about using the parts of animals to replace those which have broken down in the human. Such unhealthy thoughts have arisen from the same egocentric views which Victorian forefathers hurled at Darwin over a hundred years ago. In some people it is simply their squeamishness which prevents them making a rational decision to permit bits of their empty bodies to help others live less painful and fuller lives. The time is long overdue for all dead bodies, of whatever age, to be made available for use to help the living, and laws should be drawn up to that effect. To enable minds to become adjusted there could be initially, for a minimum period only, the ability for individuals, not families, to opt out.

Only such an act would provide sufficient organs to save lives as even in the developed countries people are still dying or leading lives of great distress, pain and fear, from the lack of organs to transplant caused by society's misplaced regard for their dead bodies. So as the 1990s begin Man is faced with a moral dilemma where it is acceptable for those driven by love to give up one of their own kidneys for use by their loved ones, but it is immoral for them to do so for money which they could spend on other medical treatment necessary to save the life.

If the world had followed the example of those over-faithful sects who deny their children life-giving blood transfusions or vaccination against fatal diseases, many of them which have been eradicated or tamed would still be claiming lives today. The sad thing is that such life-saving treatment, part of normal everyday life in most developed countries, is not available to the poor of underdeveloped nations and such diseases which have not yet been eliminated from the world can reappear in a more virulent form. The 1980s brought widespread fear from a new killer virus which brought the scourge of AIDS, the Acquired Immune Deficiency Syndrome, which destroys the body's ability to resist illnesses and diseases and once developed brings early death. Whilst scientists search desperately for a vaccine and cure no-one knows the true extent of the spread of the virus, which may yet bring death on a horrendous scale. If it were necessary to use dead bodies to find a cure, who would deny their use?

So work continues to prolong the life of individuals. No-one wants to die except those who can no longer see a reason to live. No-one wants to think of death, it is morbid, it is sobering, it is inevitable. But there is immortality isn't there?

Yes, immortality could be a certain goal for Mankind but it will not be the inbuilt picture he has of floating on clouds playing a harp. Immortality will be here on earth. Putting aside, for a moment, fear, revulsion or any moral objections, consider what would happen to individuals if it were possible to transplant a complete brain from an old worn out body to a younger, healthier one. From the outside, to all intents and purposes, will be the same young person. But from inside looking out would be the old person with all the old memories from faces and places to ideas and ideals. Indeed if only that part of the brain which carries the memory were transferred there would still be an old head on young shoulders. Taken one step further, if it were then possible to keep transferring the same memory from one body to another over a period of thousands of years would that individual not have achieved immortality? So the question arises – is immortality simply the ability to transfer the memory for ever whilst the carrier wears out from time to time and has to be replaced? This definition of immortality is one which everyone can see and understand and one which lies within the attainment of Man.

Unlike organ transplants, unheard of fifty years ago but now commonplace, the idea of depriving some person of his complete brain, regardless of its state, to make way for another is understandably abhorrent to all. It would wipe out one person from their loved ones as the new brain would not recognize them whilst the body, the outward display, would still be the one they loved. That, in itself, would cause enormous grief and pain while the ethics of such action would not be acceptable to anyone. But if there were a painless and natural way to pass the memory from one body to another – what then?

The brain is a source of all thoughts and feelings, being connected to every part of the body. Only nature itself can produce such a complex computer which can adjust, in an instance if necessary, to any situation. All around the world, every single day of the year, the miracle of the birth of another human being takes place. In each case relatives and friends can see that the outside of the infant carries many of the physical characteristics of the parents. Older relatives of the child can see the baby's features also reflect other family members such as uncle, aunt, grandparents or even earlier ancestors. Thus, the colour of eyes, the shape of ears, nose, chin, hair colour and many other features are all family traits passed down over hundreds or even thousands of years. Bone structure, size, weight and malformations are also passed from generation to generation.

Families become aware that many other traits are heredi-tary. This can vary from bodily diseases and illnesses as well as those of the mind. Gestures and actions too are not something learned from the parents but can be seen to be family traits transmitted from one generation to the next. Even those actions or gestures of parents disliked and rejected by the young have, as they have grown older, crept, unknowingly and despite themselves into their own actions.

It is only in the lifetime of the present generation that the computer age has developed into a rash of machines which one way or another affect the lives of millions of people. In developed countries they have rapidly become part of every-day life for all working people. Experience about what com-puters do brings a better understanding of how the brain operates like a super-computer sending its signals to all parts of the body in accordance with its set programme, mostly without the individual being aware of it. The restless movements of arms and legs, the beating of the heart, breathing, seeing, hearing, and thousands of other functions take place automati-cally. Such movements include family traits of tapping the fingers, twisting locks of hair, biting fingernails etc., etc. Similarly the physical appearance of the unborn child is programmed into the memory. A slight malfunction of the brain computer will change the baby's appearance so that the full likeness of the parents is not so apparent. The brain is also the centre of thought and intellectual power in Man and it controls the processes of sensation, learning and memory.

Individuals can see both the outward appearances of their body as well as their inner feelings and can recognize some of them as coming from their parents or grandparents. Stories from the latter tells parents how the actions of their children follow many of their own childish habits when crawling, talking and eating. Other family traits such as left-handedness, needing eye correction, going prematurely grey haired, are also apparent.

Hidden traits are more difficult. Being oversexed or frigid, being aggressive or over-protective, being violent or loving, being crooked or honest, being angry, tearful, claustrophobic, frightened of fluttery things, bats, mice, the need for the excitement drug – all the development of mental facets which are carried from generation to generation. Thus all the physical and mental processes from which attitudes develop come from individual's memories carried into the new born brain. And somewhere, also disconnected from the conscious mind, will be other memories held within its store.

It is this separation between the conscious and sub-conscious minds which does not allow Man to knowingly recall the memories of his forefathers but signs can be seen that such memories carry anger, dislike and even hatred possibly over hundreds of years. These memories may be responsible for driving people to follow in fathers footsteps or to yearn, often unknowingly, for something from the past. It explains why everyone experiences those intriguing flashes of *deja vu* which will send them searching their minds trying to grasp at air until the experience floats away and is lost. How frustrating it is when individuals are aware that their minds hold information which they are unable to recall. It is strange that they know, without doubt, when the information is there and that, given a jog, the brain, computer like, will remind them of that knowledge.

Hypnotists are able to plumb the memory banks because they go to the unconscious mind where the information lies. There are stories of them being able, in some cases, to delve beyond the birth of the individual but Man's scepticism and mistrust of his fellow cannot allow acceptance of such stories. But they can accept that by entering sub-conscious minds they are able to plant some thought which compels the individual unknowingly to act out later. For they have seen that under hypnosis people can be made to dance, sing or perform freely acts which, in their conscious state, they would not have done. The victim can be made to respond at any time to a command which can be triggered by a sound or action and then carry out the command which the hypnotist placed in their minds without question and without being aware that they are being manipulated. That this can happen must beg the question about how much of individual's minds are driven in a similar way by thoughts and ideas of their ancestors?

There are many activities which need to be looked at again in this way. Examples are those cases of abuse or unprovoked violence to children by those who experienced such traumas in their own childhood. Studies indicate such people are more likely to inflict the same pain on their own children but is this due to their earlier experiences or to an inherited compulsion?

There are also those wonderful true life stories that appear from time to time of individuals who, without any lessons or even previous interest, suddenly, when confronted with a musical instrument, play it quite brilliantly. Even the music they play is not something which has been knowingly known to them before. Genuine cases which involve the mentally handicapped, the blind and the deaf are particularly fascinating. Similarly there are many, many cases of young children whose brilliance is way ahead of their contemporaries. Society calls them gifted, and so they are, but it is possible that, like the sudden musician, these phenomenon are due to their ability to call on past knowledge inherited from ancestors.

Occasionally the recall becomes too real and results in the plight of those people who claim to be reincarnated. Throughout the decades there are individual cases of lives, actions and eras vividly recalled from the past. Such detailed recollections are extremely frightening to those involved and they become isolated, disbelieved by those whose support they most need. Many have been locked away in asylums because no-one, sometimes not even they themselves, could understand.

Everyone dreams but can rarely recall them. However,

somehow, individuals are aware that they have recurring dreams in which they have visited the same large house, or town, or country which in their dreams was intimately known to them and unquestioningly accepted as if it were part of their lives. In such dreams the story repeats itself exactly as if being played back on a video tape. Are such dreams, and indeed other pictures that pass through the mind during sleep which seem disconnected from the lives and worries of this life, another memory from the past?

Many people are aware that they have some compulsive action or uncontrollable habit while others may not recognize them as such. But they exist and so suggest that, in much the same way as the hypnotist plants thoughts and ideas into the subconscious mind to be acted upon later, so the lives and actions of individuals are governed by those thoughts and ideas of their ancestors, whose memories they carry and pass on in turn through their seeds to their own children. Individuals should keep full diaries of their feelings and actions to pass on to their children and grandchildren so that they may know what lies in their subconscious minds. For it is the inbuilt memory system within individuals which not only performs functions automatically but will drive the conscious mind into actions that it may not wish to take. We are all aware of how our memories dim with time but if we were able to connect our conscious thoughts with past memories locked deeply in the subconscious mind it could enable us to recall past lives for hundreds, or even thousands of years.

Bringing together the live mind with thoughts from past ancestors could be the everlasting life promised by the God of the Bible for it is to him that the Man must turn to find his past and his future, for that God was the creator of Man.

Man must look at his own recorded history of the world to see that throughout the ages there are several examples of intrepid explorers going into the unknown to seek fame and fortune. When new worlds have been discovered groups of like minded people have left their homelands behind in their search for a land where they may have the freedom to follow their beliefs, each clutching his own dream for a better life.

The Bible references make it clear that God came from the heavens. There is little doubt that among the billions and billions of stars in those heavens there are other habitable planets which, with Man's limited knowledge, are currently far beyond his reach. There can be little doubt that, in the fullness of time, spacecraft will be launched into the unknown in much the same way as the little ships of history cast off from shore to enter uncharted waters and face unknown dangers. In the latter part of the twentieth century spacecraft have left earth to search for the possibility of new worlds in the cosmos and their discovery will stimulate expeditions to leave earth to investigate them.

But, because of the enormous distances involved, the time spent travelling to any new planet could literally be a lifetime. Long distance space travel would require significant advances on Man's present state of the art, requiring must larger ships that could travel a good deal faster than they can today. But, in due time, exploration of space beyond the solar system will become a reality and it is certain that the very discovery of another habitable planet would, compulsively, cause Man to investigate. Imagine the excitement if an early unmanned craft sent back information that the planet was made up of a mixture of water and land which was covered with vegetation with an abundance of inhabitants, all primitive. Imagine the disappointment were Man to learn that some major ingredients of the planet such as the air mixture, atmospheric pressure, or both, were toxic to him and he could only survive there in life-support suits or in special buildings.

Nevertheless he would want to inhabit the new planet for it is in his blood to run away to escape to a new world where he feels he will be able to set his own priorities. Meanwhile during the long years of waiting for the craft to reach its destination and send back the results of planned experiments the world's problems would march inexorably on with the serious shortage of resources on earth, exacerbated by overcrowding, making matters worse. The world's scientists, possibly separately as now, would launch major studies of the problems of the new planet to see how the environmental differences could be overcome. Once the possibility of Man's life being tenable on the planet was established it would not take long to arrange an advance party of scientists to be despatched to prepare the way for colonization.

The major problems which could prevent this would be the limited number of people that could be transported at any one time, their life-span compared with the journey time and how to control childbirth to avoid overcrowding on the one hand or deletion of a viable number of adults on the other. But there is another way. It is no longer necessary to speculate about Man being able to keep his fertile seeds in deep freeze and later implant them into the womb to produce normal healthy babies since this is another of Man's recent achievements. Further research will enable him to keep his seeds indefinitely in their frozen state. With an ability to carry forward his memory within his seed it would be possible to transfer large numbers of people over any time and distance in a state of suspended animation using a very small space. The main problem facing the advance party during their travels and on arrival would be finding sufficient wombs in which to plant the seeds where they could safely remain for the nine month gestation period.

Some time later a second wave of scientists, carrying the all-important seeds, could undertake a follow-up research pro-gramme based upon the advance party's work to iron out many of the problems, knowing that more trials would be necessary on their arrival on the new planet. The great difficulties caused by the two major problems of a toxic environment and the need for sufficient wombs could be overcome by using the existing animals of the new planet to carry Man's fertilized seeds as surrogate mothers. It would be necessary to introduce many of the features of the existing animals' genetics into the infants to enable their survival to be assured. The risks would be measured and considered very deeply, the research teams having very much in mind that the progeny would be carrying a human brain with Man's me-mory and intelligence, and that could turn out to be disastrous if the Man and animal mixture was not perfect. The leader of the expedition sent to establish a new world would have been told before he left that no real knowledge or power should be allowed to pass to the new race until they had proved their ability and could be trusted not to misuse it.

During the long journey to the planet the leader's tasks would be to prepare the team on board for the work ahead. They would be fully aware that they would be faced with the straight options of destruction or survival. The success of the expedition would fail if they held religious and moral views similar to those firmly planted in the minds of twentieth century Man. They would know that they were creating thinking beings which, if they threatened their future, would have to be destroyed.

The team themselves would, like immigrants of the past, leave their homelands behind them taking their families with them as the journey would take several years to complete. It is not possible to imagine the excitement and anticipation as they neared journey's end with everyone gripped with apprehension, looking forward with great trepidation to their arrival on the new planet and the end of their mammoth journey. The results from expeditions which preceded them would have confirmed and enhanced the information from the early unmanned craft that a tremendous variety of plant and animal life, all primitive, were waiting for them. In this new land they, as the first animal capable of cohesive thinking, would be God.

At this part of history Man is now poised to pick up the story where the Bible begins. For the new world that the expedition was about to inhabit was earth and the expedition leader was about to become the God of the Bible.

5

The ghost of Captain Cook and his voyages to new worlds would be hovering in the back of the minds of present day Man were he to handle an expedition to inhabit another planet. Unlike Cook however the space travellers would have a great deal of information about their destination. Nevertheless the feelings of the explorers as they approached for landing after a lifetime of travelling through space, their world confined to the craft itself, would have been of indescribable ecstasy.

Without doubt everyone on board would be impatient to set foot on land again and look upon the real beauty of their new planet, to see first hand the myriad of colourful plant and animal life which they had studied during their flight from the pictures sent to them by the advance party. Their happiness during the actual descent from the ship onto the new planet would scarcely be marred by the knowledge of their inability to run free; feeling the breeze they could see rustling the tall trees or smell the air of the planet which was poison to them. But the beauty of their new home, the profusion of edible animals and vegetables, the richness of an untouched wealth of minerals, and the knowledge that they had no adversaries and thus the freedom to do anything they wished, would fill them with divine feelings.

Their determination would have invigorated their desire to be reborn into a body which could run free on the new planet. They, under the direction of the advance party, would have already done a lot of work towards this end. The advance party would have highlighted the fact that visits around the globe outside the spacecraft were limited, being restricted to spacesuits, and this was causing great stress from heartache and frustration. This too would have hardened their determination to colonize the planet. The years of discussions which would have taken place before the first expedition was launched would have been based upon the information from the un-manned craft which would have been regularly updated. The exchanges between the first and second wave of explorers would have strengthened their understanding that there were hard times ahead and very tough decisions would have to be made without any equivocation or procrastination if they were to succeed.

The task facing them, that of establishing a new race, would have been formidable and would, initially, call for all experimental progeny to be subjugated. This was not to be a short term exercise, but one on which depended the survival of the people from the old planet who were asleep in the frozen seeds which the second expedition carried. More directly their success was necessary for their own survival. They would recognize an overriding need for very strict rules for the control of the new race development programme to see that nothing got out of hand or threatened the overall plan to inhabit the planet. They would also recognize the need to rigidly enforce those rules. The scientists would have further work ahead of them examining the planet's animals to confirm the work which had been done by the advance party and themselves during the long journey. Their work would have been geared to finding which animal had the greatest potential to carry their seed. The selected animal would have been as physically similar to themselves as possible to avoid any dramatic traumas when the brain perceived the new body for the first time.

All their objectives would have been established and set out long before they left the old planet. The extensive programmes of research would have involved many people in many years of work. The decision on the selected animal would have stood out in the records of the explorers as achieving the first major milestone in their programme to create a new body for their minds. Their record would be similar to that written in the Bible which says:

'Let us make man in our image, after our likeness.'

The need for subjugation was essential. The immigrants were about to create a race which had the ability to reproduce itself and could, unless controlled, in a relatively short space of time outnumber them. Thus they had to establish from the very beginning that the new race would unquestioningly follow their orders. One of the team, probably the leader, would be the master of the new race, demonstrating by fear and superstition that he was the Lord of all creation.

Planting the seeds of extremely intelligent beings from one planet into the womb of primitive animals from another which has a very different atmosphere, would have been, to say the least, a very hazardous experiment. The risks would have been worsened by the necessity of introducing into the new progeny some part of the seed carrying animal to neutralize the environmental differences. The scientists would have planned to avoid, at all cost, the disastrous consequences of a failure and would have needed to enforce a rigorous policy to destroy without hesitation any mutation which would threaten their goals for a satisfactory vehicle for their minds and knowledge. Each infant would have been kept under very close scrutiny and tight controls of their development would be applied. It was probably necessary to make physical changes to the brains of the new race to ensure that the level of intelligence was initially measurably lower than that of their masters but higher than that of their primitive surrogate mothers.

The race of New Man would have been required to operate within extremely strict rules which the team would have devised during their flight to earth and any attempt at deviation would have been met with instant and heavy punishment. The rules would become the law.

From the genetic similarities that can be seen by today's scientists the primates were finally selected by the newly arrived overlords as the surrogate mothers for their seeds. Many experiments would have been conducted with hundreds, probably thousands, of failures which would be sacrificed in the search for a perfect carrier. Once the teams had produced a specimen which behaved in a manner acceptable to them Man would have been created and that man became Adam of the Bible.

From that moment every birth, marriage and death would have been carefully recorded while sex between them would have been restricted upon pain of death, to allocated partners. To avoid confrontation with great numbers of people which may, by oratory and argument, be whipped to opposing or violent action, a spokesman would be appointed through whom the overlords would issue their commands. He would be the only one, without special permission to the contrary, to

63

approach the Lord. In this way the Gods could exercise their powers from a distance and sustain the mystique and fear which they needed to maintain control.

The Bible records actions similar to these including listing the genealogy, or who begat whom, of the descendants of Adam. The books of Moses show how the Gods dealt with him as the spokesman of the new people and shows how the laws were established. One of the first orders to be issued by God was that he was the only God, totally in charge, and thus the only one able to issue commands. If twentieth century Man were setting off to establish himself on a new planet which was inhabited only by primitive animals would he act differently?

Does this concept, which has surfaced in differing forms from time to time, provide a better understanding of the records set out in the Bible? Indeed does it give a clearer picture of God himself? Does it explain why, when he appeared so often to Moses and his angels freely visited his people, he appears to have forsaken the world. It can and does give whole new meanings to many Bible pieces such as:

'And suddenly there came a sound from heaven as
of a rushing mighty wind, and it filled all the house
where they were sitting. And there appeared unto
them cloven tongues like as of fire.'

As with many other quotations from the Bible heaven is not depicted as a mythical place set aside for all who obey God's commands but is simply a description of space and the sky.

The concept can give a better understanding of the need for the ten commandments at that time although many may seem irrelevant or umimportant to the world today. And the use of the young women of the new race by the sons of God and the differences between the races are set out in the first four paragraphs of Genesis which say:

'And it came to pass when men began to multiply
on the face of the earth, and daughters were born
unto them.

'That the sons of God saw the daughters of men
that they were fair; and they took them wives of all
which they chose.

'And the Lord said, My spirit shall not always
strive with man, for that he also is flesh; yet his days
shall be an hundred and twenty years.

'There were giants in the earth in those days; and also after that, when the sons of God came in unto the daughters of men, and they bare children to them, the same became mighty men which were of old, men of renown.'

In the paragraphs following this bearing of children to his sons, God saw the wickedness of man and was sorry he had created him and he decided to destroy him and, for reasons not stated, the beasts, creeping things and fowls of the air. The future of the new race was saved by Noah who found grace in the eyes of the Lord. He was given instructions by God on saving himself and his family and some of the animals.

Like many other writings which must, of necessity, be after the events, the Bible stories will contain embellishments in their detail but they cannot, nor must not, be rejected as within their tomes lies the history and the future of Mankind. It is doubtful if much has been lost in the translations although there will be occasions where the modern meaning has changed from the original. But the ancient interpretations, based upon contemporary knowledge and the need to express them in ways acceptable to the world of the time, do need extensive updating. The teachings of the church need revision to eliminate fear and reduce the deliberate mystique and magic which fill their rituals. It is time to look again at the objective of immortality and not just follow the conditioned thinking which has been placed in the minds of Man for generation after generation. If Man sits and waits for someone else to change his world then it will slide inexorably into anarchy bringing violence, pain and death. Positive action must be taken to seek ways of enhancing the lives and future of all people of the world.

The concept would bring new, more understandable, meanings to the life and teachings of Jesus Christ, as the son of the God of the Bible and as recorded in the four gospels. The references to the virgin birth which puzzled our forefathers for centuries becomes understandable to today's world who have seen only recently the planting of de-frosted fertile seeds into the womb resulting in successful births. Thus, for the first time, we can picture the planting of the seed of God in Mary's womb by Gabriel, making her a surrogate mother to Christ. Man's current knowledge is placed in its comparative position when it is remembered that this event took place two thousand years ago.

Another modern development that can be seen on every clear evening particularly near airports, are the lights which skim across the sky, their movement looking so much like the rest of the stars burning brightly so many millions of miles away. The star of Bethlehem moving in a similar way marked out the stable in which Jesus was born. Following the birth of Jesus, Luke's book records an angel appearing to the shepherds carrying the news. Having given his message he was suddenly joined by a great company of the heavenly host and, after praising God, they all went into heaven. Throughout the Bible there are references of God's messengers going into or coming out of heaven. Indeed Christ himself was taken up until a cloud hid him from their sight.

Many of Jesus's miracles were healing the sick and although the doctors of today would be able to match many of them, two thousand years ago they must have been like magic. Some of Jesus's other miracles, such as commanding the wind and waves to be peaceful, may have a different explanation. In that story whilst on the lake asleep a furious storm came up without warning so that the waves swept over the boat. The gospel records that Jesus rebuked the winds and waves and they became completely calm. It is just as possible that the sudden arrival and departure of the storm could have been caused by one of Jesus's own aircraft hovering overhead and it was his own people he was rebuking for their carelessness.

There can be no doubt that Jesus's knowledge and those of his supporting angels were far in excess of his time compared to the human population. Although present day Man's knowledge has progressed, catching up in some areas to that displayed by Christ two thousand years ago, it still falls short in some areas. On the other hand, if someone with today's knowledge could travel back even a few hundred years they would themselves be miracle workers. It is however important to remember that the writers of the scriptures did not have Jesus's knowledge and needed to express themselves, if attention was to be paid to their writings, in terms which were acceptable and understandable to the people of their time.

But the importance of the Bible, or indeed other religious writings, is the message that it carries. No amount of re-interpretation of the writings or disparaging comments made in the light of Man's greater knowledge today about the miracles Jesus performed will alter that message. His reason for appearing on earth was to remind the new race of inhabitants that it was he, in one of his forefather's bodies, who created Mankind. The objective of his father remained the same, of establishing a race of people capable of love and understanding and free from hatred and petty jealousies. Only such a people could be given the full knowledge of the Gods so that memories could pass from father to son, from generation to generation. Such knowledge would give to the people of the world great power as well as immortality and they would not only need to earn it but also to demonstrate that they would not abuse it but would use it wisely and well.

Over the years the promise of immortality has been used by the churches and has come to mean that when an individual dies his body remains on earth whilst his spirit rises to heaven, or falls to hell depending on his behaviour. But throughout the gospels Jesus shows that immortality is the continuation of memory, not an everlasting body. He refers many times to the fact that he and the father are one. The churches themselves worship God as a trilogy, God the father, God the son and God the holy ghost. The book of John sets out in chapter three one of Jesus's explanations where it tells of Nicodemus, a member of the Jewish ruling council, speaking with him saying:

'Rabbi, we know you are a teacher who has come from God. For no one could perform the miraculous signs you are doing if God were not within him.

'In reply Jesus declared, "I tell you the truth, unless a man is born again, he cannot see the kingdom of God".'

Jesus tried to explain many times that he had not come to condemn but to save, almost begging the people to listen. Often the crowds to whom he spoke got angry and tried to seize or stone him but each time he escaped. Many trips had to be undertaken in secret for fear of his life. His frustration with the world must have been great, for everyone at some time or another finds themselves in the position where those around do not believe what they are being told. One of many examples of Christ's frustration can be seen in John's gospel where he said to those Jews who were stoning him:

'Why then do you accuse me of blasphemy be-

67

cause I said "I am God's Son"? Do not believe me unless I do what my Father does. But if I do it, even though you do not believe me, believe the miracles, that you may learn and understand that the Father is in me, and I in the Father.'

Two promises were made in the Bible for future generations to note; the return of the son of God to earth, and a day of judgement. On that day:

'The Son of Man will send out his angels, and they will weed out of his kingdom everything that causes sin and all who do evil.'

Religions teach that on the day of judgement every person who has ever lived will be called upon to give an account of himself to God. But individuals cannot isolate themselves from what contemporaries have done and thus they will have to account for the era in which they lived and the part they played in it. Turning away from atrocities because the sight is too horrible to contemplate, or feeling horror or revulsion against the act will not be an answer which would satisfy God. Many of Hitler's nazi sadists who put millions to death in every degradable way claimed they did not agree with what they were doing but were acting under orders and thus unable to do anything about it; but their fellow men, in the form of legal courts, condemned them. Does anyone really believe that on the day of judgement individuals will not have to answer for the state of their world, for if they are not responsible for it who is?

The decision to be made by God on the day of judgement will be whether human beings can be trusted to be given the secret of his great powers, including the ultimate knowledge to enable the father to live in the son by passing memory and knowledge from generation to generation. On that day it will be the *living* human race who will be called upon to justify what it has done to deserve that trust with the prize of immortality depending upon the answers.

6

As God views the state of the world and the actions of its people, what will he think? Will he understand, for example, the killing and maiming undertaken in his name by those blinded with hatred which has been stirred up by religious differences? Will he forgive those who lament the killing and maiming and other unspeakable horrors that have been going on around the world but have done little or nothing but moan. In many parts of the world it is the people who elect the governments and thus they have power in their hands to say and do something.

So how would the human race sum up its behaviour in the twentieth century to God. Two world wars and over the forty-five years since the end of the second the world has been littered with mountains of corpses in one country after another. In many African states such as Angola, Biafra, Ethiopia, Uganda and others. In Asian Korea, Vietnam, Kampuchea, Afghanistan and others. In the Middle East, Iran, Iraq, Lebanon, Palestine and others. In Cyprus and Aden. In the Americas, the Falklands, Nicaragua and others. In Christ's own town of Jerusalem and the surrounding area where he preached peace and love there is hatred and violence, while total anarchy seems to have taken root in the adjacent state of Lebanon. Alongside them the religious related Iran/Iraq war had grown more violent, more full of hatred as it progressed. Such hatred has exhibited a horrible ecstasy in killing and hurting in any way, preferably by causing as much pain and suffering as possible. Chemical weapons, which should have no place in a sane world and should have been banned as soon as their horror was discovered, have bitten deeply into the flesh of their victims who have included babies not yet able to think, let alone hate, and have scarred deep into the souls of their close families. And the human race, all over the world, watched.

69

Despite the smallness of the world few people of the richer nations could pin-point Kampuchea, formerly Cambodia, where fighting and inhuman abuse was inflicted upon a people who lost a quarter of their population in what must be the largest case of genocide ever. It only ended with the expulsion of the Khmer Rouge by the neighbouring army of Vietnam who occupied the country for ten years. During that period the people of Cambodia have been internationally denied any development aid by the United Nations who have continued to accept the Khmer Rouge as the representatives of the Cambodian people. When the Vietnamese troops withdrew in the latter half of 1989, despite pleas from the frightened, helpless Cambodians, the vicious Pol Pot's Khmer Rouge regime returned from their safe haven across the border with Thailand to continue their genocidal holocaust where they left off. No protests by world leaders, no preventive action, no help for the people. The extent of the infamy, suffering and unspeakable horror that is going on in that country is relatively unknown, apparently unmourned by a world of people unaffected by the tragedy. For the Cambodian people there is no hope, they have been deserted by an uncaring world which seems oblivious to the terror they have had to undergo every day of their wretched lives.

Of course world leaders are aware of the scale of the disaster besetting these poor people, and although anyone with the tiniest touch of feeling cannot fail to be moved by their plight, they do nothing. Neither do you. Neither do I. It is time we questioned what our governments have been doing in our name for while they are part of any ban on aid, so are we. They act for us so make no mistake, by our apathy we are all as guilty as they are. Why is there no aid? Cynics are suggesting that United States bitterness against Vietnam is responsible for this terrible inhuman disregard of life. Surely not. It is a tragedy that such suggestions have any credibility but mistrust is now so deep that they have. And Britain is one of those countries which are supporting such actions.

But our governments have taken us to war for less. The United Nations have sent in troops as peacekeepers in other parts of the world for less. If Vietnamese troops can hold the peace, why not the United Nations? What is happening in this God forsaken country? Do you know what your government is doing in that area? I cannot say that I have seen such matters explained in any political manifestos on which we elect our representatives, so who gives them the mandate to act on life and death matters on this massive scale? It is time we insisted they answer for their actions, and truthfully.

More publicized in Britain are those problems in Africa. People all around the world have been moved by television pictures which have shown millions of people of skin and bone starving to death in East Africa, Sudan, and other countries and they have dug into their pockets to provide funds to buy food for these poverty stricken people. A dedicated few have given their lives to help and many millions owe their continued existence to such kind people. But even their help was frustrated, moving them to tears of desperation and anguish, as they have had to watch, face to face, millions of people, men, women, and particularly children, dying because of the refusal of one of the sides in the conflict which is wrecking the countries to allow safe passage to the transport which carries life. All these problems can only be solved by governments acting together to put an end to senseless killing. It must be stopped before Man gets too much of a taste for it and needs yet more terrifying horrors to satiate his lust.

Leaders of the major nations in particular have not just the future of their own nation in their hands but that of Mankind. They must stop assuming their dogma is unimpeachable. They must stop providing the support to any killers of one side or the other in countries where so many innocent lives are lost in political and religious battles. Rather there is a desperate need for them to take positive joint action to save lives, the first one being to dry up the supplies of arms and ammunition to those countries torn apart by civil war. At last, at long last, the economics of such unnecessary and irresponsible horrors inflicted upon another sector of the human race has made those nations providing political and financial support slowly, painfully slowly, aware of the futility of such long drawn out and indecisive wars. At long last, they are beginning to see that the cost in human degradation, grief and suffering is too high a price to pay for nothing. Why, oh why has it taken so long?

God would not be impressed by this record. Neither would he be impressed by claims that the world has had to learn its lesson the hard way and that there is a glimmer at last, after

71

millions and millions of deaths, it is being learnt. Time may not be on the side of the human race in this matter. The signs are that at this moment in its history the world is better placed than it has ever been to grasp peace firmly by the hand. Failure to do so would be catastrophic.

Forty-five years after the end of the second world war the peoples of the nations are split into two groups; those who did not experience the true horrors that were unleashed during that war, Man against Man, who are able to view the actions in a detached manner, and those in whose living memories the pain, horror, fear and distress were etched deep in their hearts and minds. It is people in the latter group who saw, amidst the anguish, a comradeship, a tremendous spirit of joint affection, tolerance and understanding, and true friendships within the community with stranger helping stranger. Short shrift was given to anyone engaged in activities which detracted from the war effort or which caused further pain unnecessarily. Even in the rich language of English, words could not express the truly wonderful experience which existed in the communities in those times. Those that lived through the disaster and pain of war mourned the passing of that spirit which cut across social and national barriers.

This spirit was fostered by nations being fed with information in such a way to encourage their efforts and hold up their morale, cheering the goodies and booing the baddies. They were in no doubt who the enemy were, and politics and other differences were forgotten or ignored in the fight to defeat that enemy. In that spirit, weapons of death were sent from America and Britain to their Russian allies. What a pity weapons of life could not be so freely given in the search for peace. Persuasion is one of Man's most powerful weapons but even that has been misused. Look, for example, how Hitler persuaded the usually strong-minded German people into war. But truth must be the watchword. If governments and news media would give a balanced report of the facts without rancour, innuendo, wild accusations, xenophobia, lies or insidious insinuations, there may be a chance that such a spirit could be rekindled on a world wide basis. Then, and then only, God may be convinced that the world means business. In a few years the leaders of nations will be those born after the world wars, and although they will know from their country's history about the atrocities which befell their people, they will not know of this tremendous spirit talked about by their elders far more than the pain, now diluted with time. When the human race looks to its common aim and throws off its ancestral legacy of attitudes and pre-programmed reactions such a spirit will rise again. But it won't happen by itself, we cannot continue to drift.

Before the manufacture of the atom bomb and the raising of the iron curtain, the brutal activities of any tyrant who set himself up as the leader of a nation was curtailed by the larger nations of the world. Since then the two major super powers of the USA and the USSR, with their politics poles apart, have supported any national leader, however much of a murdering megalomaniac the individual is, who seeks their help by declaring himself, and his country of course, in opposition to the other power.

But America, the self-declared world's most powerful nation, met its Waterloo in the tiny country of Vietnam while Russia, reputed to have an even greater war machine, met its in the hills of Afghanistan. As with several other bloody civil wars, mostly in countries which could ill afford to feed their people, they have grown progressively more violent and unquenchable. Sadly the poor people of those countries were in the centre of the horrors which were simply the superpowers battling against each other, often one of them by proxy. Their minds remain packed with the memories of fifty years ago when both nations were attacked without warning engulfing them in the ongoing second world war. Neither is prepared to let it happen again and with each fearful of the other, an arms race has ballooned and eaten up massive resources which could have been used to improve not only the standard of living of their own people but those of the poor of the world. It is tragic that on this small planet in the 1990s some nations' children are reaching adulthood never having known peace. Who is responsible for them being brought up with hatred in their hearts and killing in their souls? Is it not past time that the most powerful nations of the world worked together, each with their allies, to end such horrors?

In the past few years sanity has entered the world with the arrival of one man centre stage. Mikhael Gorbachev has devastated the lies which had been fed to his people since the second world war ended. His overtures for peace have produced substantial reductions in the world tension as well as in weaponry itself. He has withdrawn his army from Afghanistan recognizing, perhaps quicker than America did in Vietnam, the futility of it all. He is demonstrating a wish for his people to have improved standards of life by looking towards withdrawing Soviet support in other war ravaged areas of the world. His main concern is that Western leaders do not try to capitalize on his actions, thus undermining his peaceful endeavours. There is a long way to go and there is a golden opportunity for the human race to work together to embrace this moment in history, for God will never forgive any failure to act now.

In his short time on the world's stage Gorbachev has done more for peace than any national leader. He has had to throw away fifty years of bigotry and distrust which his people had learned from the very hard lesson of an unprovoked attack in the second world war and which they have been taught to guard against every since. With this breath of fresh air entering the Kremlin all world leaders must put aside their personal feelings and look towards what is best for the world. The rewards are far too great to allow individual's need for importance or to delay progress to peace by taking rigid stances on principle. It matters not which of the several claimants can take credit for what is happening in the attitude of a very powerful nation, the greater goal of peace is visible and it must be of prime and overriding importance. For those nations which branded Russia as an aggressor forty years ago and have since trained their 'defence' effort to fight them as the main enemy, now is the time for change. For the West can see Gorbachev's *Glasnost* working as the Soviet Union relaxes her tight grip on her member nations, Poland, Hungary, East Germany etc., are all demonstrating that openness that Gorbachev has introduced. The West must embrace the new era by helping him achieve an early success in improving the standard of living for his people. His gain will be ours. We must see that he gets full recognition for what he has done for world peace and emulate his example.

Typically for Man, but tragically for the human race, as war has become futile it has been replaced by something much more insidious, much more intangible, bringing with it an even greater fear than the threat of nuclear holocaust. This is another affront to humanity that grows more terrible each day. The hatred which is overpowering individuals is driving them to satiate their blood lust, no longer caring who is killed or maimed. Bombs are planted in public places and the time fuse selects its targets indiscriminately. Many of the terrorist organizations have spokesmen or political representatives or other supporters in public life who give respectability to cold blooded murderers and their activities. National boundaries permit murderers to go free and thus, in both ways, terrorism is actively encouraged. Like the school bully, if their vicious behaviour is not nipped in the bud it will take over and the majority will succumb to terror from a very small minority. Without active financial support terrorism will die. Who then is responsible for its continuation?

The world must not miss its opportunity for peace by default. There are desperate cries for help from the people of the poorer nations whose governments are spending their totally inadequate resources on arms and ammunition to fight civil wars. There are desperate cries from the people of the richer nations to divert funds spent on preparations for war to more social needs. Neither can be achieved without world cooperation and this objective can only be achieved through trust.

But vacillation must stop and action must be take for, when God returns on that day of judgement and looks upon his human race they will have to be in a far, far better position to answer his question than they are now; whether they are fit to receive the blessings of his knowledge and the gift of immortality.

Looking at today's world through his eyes how would the human race answer that question? Is there any individual anywhere in the world who would be prepared to speak up for the whole human race? Is there any individual anywhere in the world who would be prepared to ask for such power to be placed in the hands of fellow man without massive radical changes in the way his race are mismanaging the world?

The concept of God coming from another world is not new. Many words have been written about the possibility of aliens visiting earth which have been disregarded or belittled by those whose thinking follows deeply ingrained channels. Yet thousands of millions of people believe that Christ himself was

75

accompanied by angels from heaven with knowledge well in advance of his time. Where did they come from? Where did they go?

In the beginning when God created Man with an intelligence above that of the animal kingdom but well below his own he would want to see how Man used his powers before increasing them. Before he left the planet he would want to leave knowledge in a form where it could be released slowly over hundreds or thousands of years so that Man could learn to cope with new situations. About the time of Christ there were clearly a number of angels around although it seems likely that the atmosphere was toxic to them as they had to revert to surrogate motherhood once more to get Christ on earth. At about the same time Christs helpers would be looking for ways to provide fountains of knowledge which could be released slowly to Man.

Over the centuries Man's belief in spirits has diminished but hundreds of years ago his belief was strong although it may have been the result of religious teachings. Today few profess to believe in ghosts but everyone has experienced them, often without knowing it. For the earth and its structures are drenched with messages from the past and for the future. Nowhere is Man's conditioned thinking more apparent than in the inconsistency between his beliefs in God and after-life and his refusal to believe in ghosts.

But twentieth century Man has seen the impossible happen in his time. For today unconnected and inert objects can be activated into brilliant bursts of sound and colour. Radios, televisions, record players, tape players and disc players are all ready for a signal to make them belch forth sound and vision. Some will reproduce into pre-set patterns of music or pictures from tapes or discs, others will show events in differing parts of the world as they are happening. But nothing can be obtained until the inert objects are activated by bringing together machine and tapes or discs. In all cases the magic is produced through invisible electromagnetic radiation and nothing can be achieved unless the equipment matches the signal input. And the playing machines can be set to provide sound or picture many days ahead.

The same could be said for ghosts. From rocks, earth, trees, buildings or any other structure magnetic radiation emanates which remains invisible and dormant until a matching receptor passes by. Such radiation could have been placed there by signals from one human brain and is only capable of reception by another. Very few people can use their ability to see the visual ghosts which so often seem to have resulted from some terrifying traumatic experience which would have produced immense brain wave activity. Reported ghosts always seem to follow the same ritual each time as though a recording were being replayed. Other ghostly activities such as unexplained noises, the movement of objects or levitation would all come from a change in an object's magnetic field reacting to currently immeasurable shifts in the earth's line. Our Victorian forefathers would not have accepted that it would be possible for tape to carry pictures but at least Man of the twenty-first century has the video and can therefore see the possibility of recordings on rocks, buildings, etc. This is not as fanciful as it may sound even though he has not yet made a machine to detect them.

But non-visual ghosts are experienced by everyone at some time in their life. Unexplained eerie feelings in a house, garden, wood, indeed anywhere. Houses that sing with laughter and happiness; houses that dispense gloom and foreboding; the sudden chill of an icy finger or the someone-trod-on-my-grave syndrome always at the same place; the sudden cold draft; are all manifestations of ghosts. And there are thousands more instances which individuals can recall which have produced irrational feelings of fear, of doubt or maybe of pleasure. Simply recordings on playback?

Release of knowledge would have to be, initially at least, on trickle. Too much knowledge too soon could have been dangerous to Man's future. In their search for carriers of information the angels would have sought structures which would hold the magnetic signals which would be released later. Such structures would need to be unusual enough so that the comparatively primitive Man would venerate and thus protect them. Indeed they would need to be made in such a way that he would have difficulty in destroying them. As his knowledge grew he would give them more protection whilst he searched for their origin and meaning. The pyramids, Stonehenge, the Easter Island statues, the massive stone balls of South America, the Mayan pryamidal temples, are known throughout the world because no-one can satisfactorily explain how objects of their size and weight could be moved to their present locations. Many theories have been advanced from rolling the monoliths on logs (there are no trees on Easter Island) or making slopes of earth on which to slide the rocks into position – right through to the involvement of aliens, the latter not receiving much credibility amongst scholars. But in almost every case they are seen simply as primitive Man raising a monument to his Gods in much the same way as the later builders raised cathedrals.

But there is no satisfactory explanation about where such primitive people gained the knowledge or tools to complete the job. Would there have been a better way for people of advanced intelligence to store knowledge with a timed release of information? In the fields of the differing religions such messages are seen as enlightenment and revelations of God but progress in the world of medicine, science or learning are not. Why? But with the knowledge of the 1990s it can be seen that the idea of releasing timed signals is tenable. Look at just one of the phenomenon, Stonehenge, as an example. Many books have been written with many theories about how the stones got from Wales to Salisbury Plain and why they were put there at all. But one thing common to all the books is the statement that the builders of Stonehenge had an astonishing knowledge of the movements of sun, moon and stars.

The tangible display which the people of the 1990s can see is the accurate alignment with the sun so that on mid-summers day it rises directly over the heelstone. Other people may have read about the amazingly professional building ability of its constructors nearly four thousand years ago, about a thousand years after the building of the pyramids of Egypt, Abraham was around at the time Stonehenge was built and the Israelites had not begun their exodus from Egypt with Moses. Today's world knows that the sun plays a major part in the biological clocks of the creatures, including Man, which live on earth. Thus it is easier for today's world to accept the possibility that the relationship between the magnetic fields of earth and sun, moon and stars, could cause signals to be released from such a structure with the length of the release being controlled by the gravitational changes which take place as the bodies change their positions in space.

So God could have left his knowledge to be given to

Mankind in such a form of controlled flow. As Man's knowledge grew he would be able to see more and more that the stones were placed by someone with a knowledge of building work, a knowledge of the stars, and with an ability to move massive stones hundreds of miles from their place of origin. And all this was accomplished at the time of pre-historic Man. It can be expected that Man has produced some of his own monoliths as a tribute to his God so that not all unusual structures will be rock recordings dispensing knowledge. But if Man were able to identify where the recordings lay and became able to extract the information set in them, would he achieve his ultimate goal of immortality?

Whether he can find and read such hidden signals or not the information flow will continue and he may well discover he has the ability to reconnect his memories of past lives with the body of today in a similar way to the accidental cases of reincarnated people. If he succeeds he will have enormous power which if misused could spell the end of Mankind. But it remains a strong possibility that the secret of eternal life was not placed by God in the fountains of knowledge for the Bible tells that Man will have to await the return of his creator on the day of judgement to see whether he has earned such a glorious prize.

If immortality is to mean anything at all it must mean peace throughout the world, for only with peace comes freedom and love. Action needs to be taken against the small minority of violent and criminal people who are frightening the rest but it is being retarded by those people who feel such action may affect the civil liberties of the vast majority. Such a hypothesis is dangerous and can result in the worse consequences of uncontrolled retaliatory action or by the minority ruling the majority by fear. Either way it is essential that the world puts an end to evil before it puts an end to it, for freedom and the future of Mankind are at stake.

7

Freedom is a word much misused by the human race, each protagonist using his own personal meaning which will support whatever cause he is advancing. Freedom is relative. Today Man could be on the threshold of moving in the direction of world freedom but first it is necessary to define what he means by freedom by abandoning all his pre-conceived notions of what he thinks it is and start to look at how free individuals really are. To do this it is essential for everyone to take a detached look at themselves as well as at those around them to see how tightly they are bound, partly by conditioned thinking that has been drummed into them over the centuries, partly by those animal instincts that were inherited from their earliest ancestors, and partly by external energies currently beyond human ken.

It is frightening to think that the desire of Man's creator, for Man to be as perfect as himself, may still lie in the minds of modern Man, resurfacing in megalomaniacal racial hatred and genocide like that of Adolf Hitler's nazis. Man's knowledge of the workings of mind and body are still very limited despite the rapid advances in the field of medicine over the past fifty years and although there is a growing awareness that many individuals are carried along to perform actions despite their wishes to the contrary, no-one knows the extent to which that happens. There are few individuals who can understand that people are driven to acts by compulsion. They know they can control their own actions and so refuse to accept that others cannot do the same. Thus there is no sympathy or help for anyone carrying out actions which society finds anti-social or abhorrent.

But one way or another, sometime during their life, everyone has their actions driven by fear, conformity or compulsion. The usually truthful child who may steal or lie to avoid angering father or mother whom he or she dearly loves; being unable to attend functions without wearing the clothes which the occasion demands; smoking, drinking or superstitious rituals; all are examples where choice is unavailable. Interference in thoughts and actions is often only visible to those that have them and, however much they want rid of them, society has taught them to believe that any admission that they were unable to control themselves was simply a sign of weakness on their part. Society coerces conformity. Many individuals may not even recognize their actions as compulsive and thus an infringement of their personal freedom and, even when they do, they refuse to admit it even to themselves. If they consciously feel that what they are doing is what they want to do, are they free?

Some of those who have been able to conquer their less dramatic compulsive habits gloat over those who cannot with an arrogant feeling of superiority. Because of these attitudes millions of people suffer untold pain and agonies to hide their own 'unacceptable' compulsive behaviour. It is the attitudes of society which nurture those behaviours until they consume their carriers causing them to satiate the appetite which engulfs them. Help early on in the development of compulsions could stop them reaching this stage for, regardless of what one may think, those affected are not free.

One of Man's greatest assets is his individuality and there is a need to recognize it and encourage it and not try to constrain it within unimportant rules of snobbery or intolerance. The truth is that everyone's life is affected in some measure by uncontrollable acts which show themselves in different ways from minor irritations to the wish for relief by death, the latter sometimes brought about by society's quiet condemnation. Only a fortunate few will not have experienced brief moments of apparent insanity when, either deliberately or accidentally, their passions are roused to great heights, driving them unwillingly to great depths of feeling and abnormal actions. Anger, hate, rage, stubborness, jealousy, sulking, love, ecstasy, desire, greed, lust, alcohol, gambling, work, fear, and many others can, in different people, override all rational judgements.

Individuals will know, though not so keen to admit even to themselves, that they are prone to passions which give rise to years of uncontrolled conflict within themselves, within their families, within their own society and with others. The latter

81

includes any amorphous mass of a particular nation, religious sect, or race. Such passions thrive in varying degrees in the daily lives of everyone. How many will claim their actions are free?

It is a poor soul which has not experienced the all-consuming passion of love. True love outlasts both the agonies and ecstasies that accompany it through its life. Such is its power that its carrier will sacrifice his or her life for the object of their love. Nowhere is this more apparent than in family life where parents would risk, or even give, their lives to protect their children. The trust of a young child for its parents is complete and overwhelming. Pity the individual who betrays that trust. As children reach adulthood they fall in love with strangers and give to them the same trust because they assume all men are like dad or all women are like mum. It comes as a great shock to find that they are not and this time of learning can be quite traumatic for them.

Sometimes the object of true all-consuming love pretends to return it but instead uses its power to manipulate the one in love. There is only one end to such affairs, grief, distress and pain. The more they take, the worse they receive. It is wrong to say that love is blind for, despite the strong defence people may put up about their lovers, they can see the faults but are in the grip of some force which will not allow them to do anything about it. No-one who is not under the same spell will accept that nothing can be done and so the individuals are forced to lie to their families and friends, feeling that none of them understand. Any attempts to try to convince them on matters which they inwardly know to be true only results in further inner conflict, adds to the unhappiness of the unfortunate individual, and alienates those people who they need most, the family. Those squashed in a vice grip of love are not free.

It is not for nothing that the expression 'insanely jealous' exists, for jealousy, itself born of love, has the capacity to eat right into the heart, cause extraordinary pain and actions that no-one would take if they really had a choice. Jealousy is a terrible plague which torments so many people destroying their lives by forcing them against their will to irrational bouts of rage in which they inflict mental, sometimes physical pain on those they love, cherish and trust. Those faced with this dreadful consuming passion yet free from it themselves are unable to understand it because, on the face of it, it denies their own love and shows a total lack of trust.

Slowly but surely, as the individuals who experience it watch horrified and helpless, it erodes in its wake all traces of love, trust and understanding. It eventually tears their lives apart with those afflicted still fighting it every inch of the way but failing miserably to beat it, not out of weakness, but because there is nothing they can do on their own to stop it. They are not free.

Rage is defined as violent anger and is often unleashed as much to the surprise and distress of the individual having the fit of rage as those unsuspecting people on the receiving end. Here too it is normal to refer to *uncontrollable* fits of rage. Minor fits can be seen daily on the roads where there are clear examples of actions being taken by forces outside the individual's control. The response of a driver who feels offended by another, regardless of who is to blame for the situation, is so overwhelming and immediate that it can make even the most careful drivers react extremely dangerously with an apparent almost total disregard for their own safety or that of their passengers who may be well-loved members of their family. Rage can often be activated by stupidly minor incidents which, for no apparent reason, have been blown totally out of all proportion. So, regrettably because they really were unable to prevent themselves, pain is inflicted, apparently indiscriminately and to the recipient is unforgivable. Even those having the fit, after it is over, find it impossible to justify their actions. Again, those not subject to these fierce moments of madness find it difficult, often impossible, to accept that it is not controllable because they know they are able to control their own tempers. It is just not the same thing at all and, with no two individuals having the same force driving them, is misunderstood. Just another classified weakness of the individual sufferer. Not an emotion freely chosen.

Hatred can be stirred up fairly quickly in a crowd, usually holding for a short time but can be extended by individuals being refuelled by the feelings of those surrounding them. But hatred too can reside in the heart. Such deeply impregnated hatred can squash all other feelings driving individuals to depths of depravity in defining methods of inflicting pain, fear and death to their objects of hate. Such acts plumb the depths of inhumanity and often result in the drug of exultation which requires to be fed by worse and worse atrocities which casts serious doubts upon the sanity of the individuals. Those afflicted by this soul-eating disease are not free to think rationally about the subject of their hatred.

This century has seen the freedom of sexual expression and making love has become the euphemism for sexual intercourse with partners of the same as well as the opposite sex. But intercourse has become, in many instances, a pleasure to be taken and enjoyed with anyone at any time without love but with ecstatic wallowing in temporary lust. In full flood, sexual ecstasies have called for all sorts of degrading practices which have to be fulfilled. Drugs became a necessity to depravity. Society calls such acts perversion, the definition of which, among other things, includes the word wicked and this brings the right to condemn anyone found involved in acts of perversion. Perish the thought that those condemning are ever discovered in their own perverted acts, however private they may be.

Today many perversions are nurtured, even flaunted, by those who feel beyond criticism. But far, far, too many cry tears of pain at the compulsion which forces them against their wishes to these acts of sexual pleasure. It is a brave and loving family which tries to understand that many such acts are ordered by a powerful force which takes over minds, bodies and souls to satisfy its compelling desires. As with all demanding forces this one too can, in some individuals, overpower any other consuming passions making them helpless to stop their actions even though they are deeply in love and firmly believe that love is forever and would never sanely countenance risking the irreplaceable happiness of their family love.

Sex is probably the most powerful driver of men and can in an instant pull them magnet-like to destroy their lives and their precious love. There is no more beautiful experience on earth than love given and returned and yet it can be thrown away for a few brief moments in life, satisfying an irresistible urge rarely freely chosen.

Man's knowledge is inadequate for individuals to understand what it is that drives people from all nations and all walks of life to the self-destructive actions of all of these, and several other passions. Only those who have experienced them at full flood can understand that, while hating themselves for their actions, they are unable to stop themselves until it is too late. In extreme cases they may know they need help and desperately desire to share their troubles with the one person above all others who knows, understands and loves them. But they feel they have betrayed the unquestioning trust of their partners, parents or family and the consequential inner conflict tears them apart until their character changes beyond recognition. The pages of the agony aunts reflect some of the minor instances of cries for help and the replies tell them what they do not want to hear, that loved ones will not understand so do not confide in them and just ignore the guilt which is so insistently eating at their very souls. Major problems rarely appear in the columns because the advice will be to seek help, but from whom if the loved ones will not be able to deal with the minor problems?

With individuals all being different each will have their own normally dominant emotion. In one love may conquer all, in another jealousy can override every other emotion, in a third life is ruled by hate, and so on. But even those normally dominant emotions can, despite themselves, be over-ridden by sudden temporary uncontrollable urges, impulses or compulsions. Often it is possible for individuals and their parents to recognize the normal dominant emotions and the major over-riding short term emotions as being that of their ancestors, referred to as the family traits. Do such hereditary traits really allow the individual freedom of action?

Interference of the mind becomes more apparent and direct to most people when they watch the ability of hypnotists to place a programmed response into the minds of individuals which can be activated later by a word or action. Some commentators on the present knowledge of hypnosis say that only a small percentage of willing victims can be hypnotized and they cannot be made to carry out actions which are against their principles. It is pertinent to note that individuals can be commanded to forget that they were hypnotized and to remember nothing about what had been planted in their minds. Thus they would be unaware that their actions were anything but normal and they would therefore be unaware they were being manipulated, satisfied their actions were of their own free choice. Other authorities say that hypnotism could be responsible for many unexpected suicide cases.

Thoughts and ideas leading to actions can also secretly be placed in the mind by subliminal messages such as fast pictures which the eye cannot see or speech which the ear cannot detect. Such messages have been used in department stores, supermarkets and the like, as well as in unseen film and television commercials to place thoughts and ideas into customers' heads without their knowledge thus making them desire the product being advertised. Subliminal advertising has been banned in many countries for some years. The knowledge of it does however raise questions of whether it can be, or even is, used to promote political opinions or, in war situations, to perpetuate the war or to cause disenchantment and unrest in the foe. Its use would be limited by the ability of machines to detect such signals and slow them down to a speed which will enable them to be seen and heard.

But are there similar signals occurring naturally which causes a general change in people's feelings and actions whilst not affecting everyone? Every now and then into everyone's life comes one of those odd days when the population seem to be bent on grumbling angrily about minor matters, feeling depressed or low, or have the opposite feelings of being inexplicably happy with sunny dispositions. It is hard to believe such moods were freely chosen.

Refusal to accept that minds are being interfered with is becoming daily more difficult to justify. Man is poor in knowledge and therefore cannot understand, and too often cannot even recognize, the interference for what it is. For many millions of people however, it severely and drastically reduces their freedom of action, so much so that often life can become a living hell which can drive some individuals to seek release by death. This invasion of individual freedom takes many forms from the day to day moods which may vary from the norm for no apparent reason, to those which drive people towards slow, lingering suicide. Such interference is referred to by the medical profession under the broad heading of mental health and stress and its causes are poorly understood and treatment, except in extreme cases, is often to the body and not the mind.

Problems fall into four main groups.

There are those with irrational fears and the only control which individuals have over these horrendous life eating monsters is, if at all possible, to avoid the situations which cause them.

There are those whose lives are dictated by capricious fits.

There are those physically healthy people who experience extreme bouts of ill-health, feeling similar in many ways to drug addicts overdue for another injection but, unlike them, have no instant solution nor any understandable explanation of why they feel so terribly ill.

Finally there are those individuals who are caught in the grip of some freakish power which drives them to acts they do not want to do. Such acts can be carried out knowingly or unknowingly by the individuals.

The first of these broad groups cover many problems and are often treated, even by close and loving relatives or partners, as a matter of ridicule. By avoiding the object of their fears individuals work hard to keep them secret and avoid supercilious and pitiful looks. In those situations where it occurs the irrational fear becomes the dominant emotion killing all logical thought and sending the victims into a sickening state of uncontrolled panic. Many people with irrational fears can go through life able to avoid those situations which bring on the devastating panic although it is always at the forefront of their minds and can be brought on even by imagination.

But some problems are difficult, if not possible, to avoid and life can then be hell. Other examples such as agoraphobia, the fear of open spaces, keeps many, many people confined to their homes with the situation deteriorating as they avoid going out. A similar but reverse problem is claustrophobia, the fear of enclosed spaces, and as it keeps many out of any forms of transport and thus, their ability to move freely even day to day, they too become imprisoned in their homes and even one room of that home. Many people who declare themselves frightened of flying are really claustrophobia sufferers and cover it up because the fear of flying seems more acceptable socially. With all phobias there are differing degrees of loss of control. There are many claustrophobia sufferers for example who are able to travel in cars or on buses and trains provided the doors are not shut behind them when the panic once more sets in.

There are hundreds of such irrational fears, some partly understood others not. The fears bring panic, the heart racing till it feels it will burst, fighting for breath, an inability to think, dizziness. Such panic can be brought on by an unbelievable range of fears from the fear of a particular colour, a particular insect, fluttering things, trees, closed spaces, open spaces, thunder, lightning and other types of weather, types of vehicles, aeroplanes, diseases, illnesses or particular individuals or groups; the former can be anyone, the latter can include doctors, dentists and the like. Altogether there seems little in this world which does not bring some sort of phobia in its wake. Young people in particular do not know what is happening to them. They are unable to explain why they 'cannot' go to school. They often appear distant to their parents because they refuse many offers of wonderful trips or outings. But they are afraid of the vomiting which precedes such outings and they are in constant fear of drawing attention to themselves by being sick while out. Parents are unaware of this internal terror but even if they did the children feel, usually rightly, that such feelings will be seen as a weakness and parents will use aggression to drive out these demons which only makes matters worse and secrecy deeper.

Millions of people are affected with differing degrees of suffering. It is difficult, if not impossible, for unaffected people to understand why these abnormal fears rule and ruin people's lives. for those with more than one crippling irrational fear life becomes hopeless. None can be regarded as free.

Life is not too pleasant either for those who suffer fits. Recurrent and sudden seizures with loss of consciousness or convulsions, of fainting, paralysis, apoplexy or epilepsy, means their lives are governed by the capricious beast sitting constantly on their shoulder. The diabetic's beast is at least controllable but calls for rigid timetables and diets if fits are to be avoided. In all these cases freedom is limited by the length of the leash which contains it.

The third group covering physically fit ill people is nothing short of tragic for many. They look well and the doctors can find nothing wrong but they have illnesses. Many afflicted people have to grope their way through life trying to hide their illness grateful for any respite from tottering on the knife edge of crisis, chronic ill health. Vomiting, so frightening in the early stages, becomes just a temporary aggravation as the victim gets used to its often predictable arrival. But the truly dreadful sensation of feeling deeply ill is devastating. Those affected in varying degrees retire from life frightened that almost any tiny move from the ordinary will topple them from their knife edge into the sickening despair of ill health. And new illnesses of this kind are growing. ME, the post viral fatigue syndrome is devastating many frightened sufferers in a daily non-life struggle to survive. Even when it has been diagnosed few doctors know how to treat it.

All people in the group know they are feeling dreadfully ill though it may be difficult to describe the symptoms and cannot understand why the doctors can find nothing wrong, for until they do there seems to be no cure. The true answer is often needless or excessive anxiety about health. For many it is a vicious circle with no beginning and no end. But the symptoms are real enough and life can become very miserable for those afflicted. It can take many years for the affected individuals themselves to recognize, though not understand, what is happening, so it is not surprising that their families and friends are also puzzled. Employers lose patience with those absenting themselves so often from work with ill-defined illnesses. Everyone joins in the advice to 'pull yourself together'. The isolation of the individual just makes matters worse and he comes to the firmly held, and difficult to change, conclusion that no-one can understand his problem which becomes personal to him.

Like phobias, anxiety brings on a mass of complaints in varying degrees from simple bad health to death-seeking despair. Bouts of breathlessness, chest pains, sweating palms, dizziness and panic, all from hyperventilation, can be brought on simply by the sufferer's developed habit of thinking about his breathing. Bouts of feeling ill are also brought on by being too conscious of normal aches and pains; the fear of unexplained lumps which individuals will not take to the doctor for fear of the worst; fear of death itself; fear of feeling ill and fear of failure. Another endless list. Many try to control the physical symptoms with tranquilizers or the misuse of drugs and alcohol, which leads to worse problems, driving people to seek relief by death. Such people have no freedom.

At long last there is limited recognition of some part of this massive problem emerging in society but the concentration tends, at the moment, to be more on stress-related illnesses and groups at risk rather than on individuals. It is for the hard

89

pressed general practitioners, who themselves are generally treating the physical symptoms rather than dealing with the problem itself, to supply a medical term for the patient to use to explain to family, friends and employer why he is unwell. These terms are not always understood outside the medical world and are too often denigrated by the patient's work managers. The problems are exacerbated because such terms are wide open to abuse, being often quoted as euphemisms by those who have decided to take a day off from work for no medical reason. The true sufferers try with great determination, usually unsuccessfully, to convince themselves that they feel well. The attitudes of loved ones encourages those afflicted to avoid seeking help until it is too late. Such attitudes are the result of conditioned thinking by themselves and those around them that such matters only affect the weak and thus casts serious doubts on their characters.

The fourth group covers two types of obsessional behaviour with the important difference that one is carried out unknown to the individual whilst the other is carried out with their full knowledge but, in neither case, their full consent. Both types are extremely difficult to recognize even by the sufferers themselves. Individual cases vary from minor but irritating habits to being made to fight against all sources of help. If successful in this latter category individuals inflict a slow death upon themselves.

Some of the problems in this area of behaviour such as violence, and sexual perversions can themselves arouse irresistible fierce, basic emotional instincts, bringing a refusal to accept the possibility that individuals' sub-conscious minds may have directed the action. Many such acts carried out, sometimes with and sometimes without the individual's knowledge, are extremely offensive and often criminal. People are helpless to stem the natural anger that these cases arouse and vengeance is demanded to satisfy their feelings. The law itself recognizes some cases where the individual has done something wrong but has been totally unaware of it, but diagnosing such cases is difficult and without the necessary medical support the individuals gets no sympathy. How can society be sure that those involved in vicious and brutal attacks were able to help themselves? Could there have been a dominant emotion, sometimes brought on by drugs or alcohol, which suffocated all other feelings at the time? People who are unable to inflict physical pain on others cannot understand.

It is perhaps the shoplifting cases involving rich or famous people which receive most publicity but many people will know of a case in their own locality where previously honest and upright citizens are arrested for that offence. For the individuals involved during the first few moments of an incident, when they look all around to see who the arresting officer is talking to and realizing it is them, they think they are on the receiving end of a sick joke. They rapidly try to remember whether they have inadvertently slipped something in their pocket or bag, struggling to recall why they had entered the shop at all. The production of the stolen goods from their bag frightens and devastates them and they are convinced that someone has dropped them in there as they have no recollection of touching the items which were of no use to them whatsoever.

They wonder why the security guard insists that he had watched the event taking place. The real horror begins to dawn on the individual who is shattered, his thinking frozen in a state of disbelief. The arresting officer who witnessed the crime may scoff at such an innocent demeanour and the strong denials of the accused. To him the arrest is a triumph. It will be for others to deal with the man who was genuinely unaware of his actions and totally bewildered by the accusations. It takes months of medical treatment and police investigation before faith in him can be restored to his family. His own confidence to leave home again will take many years to accomplish and it is possible he may never recover it. The trauma following such cases is devastating to the individual and his family who, regrettably, will have to undergo smirks, scorn and pain from those who do not understand. Despite, and maybe in this narrow world because, psychiatric examination had determined that the acts were unconsciously carried out and the individual was unaware of what he had done and thus was not responsible for those actions, society sees it as a sign of weakness and condemns him, his family and his parents. Without psychiatric support his family and friends too may not understand.

There are also the less well known cases of individuals who, in a matter of a few minutes, can disappear without any

91

apparent display of unusual behaviour, to be found weeks later, hundreds of miles from home, having the time of their lives with no knowledge of what they had been doing or where they had been. These so called fugues are temporary aberrations but there are more serious cases of amnesia which last much longer and leave an individual searching for his life. He cannot recognize home, wife or family. It is difficult to imagine the distress these aberrations have on individuals and their families.

The symptoms leading to both sorts of unconscious acts, which may only become apparent after the event, can be over-dedication to their jobs and complete loyalty to their masters. Such behaviour brings the rewards of promotion and with it yet more pressures. Such unconscious acts were not taken freely.

But obsessional behaviour also covers those acts which the individual not only carries out knowingly but, in some cases, actually loiters in likely places for the opportunity to do so. After the event they may be sickened by their actions or angry with themselves for being unable to prevent them, or they may wallow in the exultation of a satiated need. But the need took over the mind and once it won the fight against the conscious mind the hunt proceeds with relish until the deed is done. Such deeds may include sexual perversions and assaults, rape, suicide and even murder. To the vast majority of people who are not driven by over-riding impulses such comments may be repugnant. They feel everyone is accountable for their actions and this is just another feeble excuse by another do-gooder feeling sorry for the poor chap who may have just beaten up and raped an eighty-year-old widow before killing her. Far from it. Something drastic must be done if the growth of such horrific crimes is to be curtailed. But society should want and demand more than that, nothing short of elimination of such crimes. Prison is not an answer. In many cases punishment itself may not be an answer.

The days of believing that everyone who knows what they are doing must accept the consequences of their actions are long gone. Such views are no longer relevant, for all around is the evidence that individuals carry out acts against themselves and the accepted norm with great secrecy and frightening dedication. One such terrible scourge is anorexia nervosa in which victims, mainly young and female, knowingly, and with a cunning of which the family would normally be proud, literally starve themselves to death. This terrible illness and the related 'gorge and vomit' bulimia nervosa caught in time can be reversed but the victim's inbuilt system of secrecy works to extraordinary lengths to avoid discovery until it's too late. The illness, for it is recognized as such, has claimed many famous and beautiful victims who, to all the puzzled bystanders, had everything to live for. Such tragic cases defy any arguments that individuals can decide their own actions and must therefore pay for them. It can clearly be seen in these cases that there is a force driving them which, if left unchecked, can destroy them. Observing the great dedication with which they pursue their objectives can their actions be said to be against their wishes? Were they freely taken?

Suicide too is knowingly carried out by victims in a state of great depression and many well-known and well-loved public figures have gone down that road of horror. So too have many friends and relatives. Society seems now to accept suicide as something that happens to those who cannot cope with life. Is it society's condemnation of them as weak-willed that prevented them seeking the help to stop them ever reaching this stage? Was suicide their free choice?

Others driven by powers outside their control are those who are unable to stop smoking, risking shortening their lives and damaging the health of their loved ones as a consequence; those who need drugs in order to live, and this may include those addicted to, or even reliant upon, tranquillizers; the compulsive eater; the alcoholic; the gambler; the flasher; the pervert; the hypochondriac; the pyromaniac; and those people whose behaviour we can only now see, has been seriously affected by diet. Into this latter category falls the hyperactive child who wreaks havoc and destruction in his path no matter what the distraught parents try to do to control him. For years such 'bad' uncontrollable children have been punished by bewildered and frustrated parents whom society blame for the awful behaviour of their children. Today science shows that what they eat and drink puts them into a conscious coma where they are unable to reason or have any real control over their actions. Yet there are still those who think that all that is needed is a good dose of discipline. Those parents whose children have been diagnosed as hyperactive have their own patience severely tested, from time to time having to determine whether fringe bad behaviour calls for firmness or is a facet of the hyperactivity, and in the very young it is often difficult to decide. As with phobias and anxieties there are many different levels and it is rare that parents or even doctors can diagnose the lower levels of hyperactive behaviour.

But such hidden problems are just the tip of a very big iceberg of hell for many. There are those poor people whose lives have been wasted, committed to caring for demanding parents who make it impossible for them to go out without distressing emotional blackmail, blanketing their enjoyment and causing deep feelings of guilt. Other people have their lives totally ruled by spouses, lovers or children. In every case the individuals are confined to their prison-homes, manipulated by jailers who play on their loyalty and love in a dreadful and cruel way. They have no freedom.

Then there are those people who have chromosome abnormalities which research has shown leads to highly aggressive and anti-social behaviour. Women are said to be of chromosome constitution XX and men of constitution XY. In the general population only a handful of men have abnormal chromosome constitutions whereas in the population of criminal and mental institutions such abnormalities show in two per cent of the inmates. Research also suggest that these abnormalities, for reasons not yet known, increase the height of individuals. A further study in criminal institutions of men of five feet eleven inches tall and over showed that one in eleven, nine per cent, of those studied had a gross chromosomal error. If this is so then their actions were being driven and they were not free.

And, despite many red herrings on the way, there is now a growing recognition that hormones play a leading role in establishing the drives of the sexes. From conception they work to promote feminine and masculine feelings so that each have inbuilt needs to fill. But women have greater senses than men, they can hear better, they notice things far more, and can detect concern in those around them which are hidden to men. To Man falls the role of manual worker at home as things mechanical are more alien to women. There are, of course, as in all matters, exceptions to all these roles, but whatever they are, they are not decided by thought but by make-up. It is interesting to ask whether the active feminists are really masculinists!

Mental illness is for most people strange, frightening and inexplicable. Even today people shun those they think may be mentally deranged. With the linking of the mental health tag to the many areas outlined comes the stigma which has been built into Man's conditioned thinking over the centuries. For he has always believed that abnormal behaviour, particularly mental abnormal behaviour, was caused by the devil or evil spirits and to this day exorcism is still practiced by churchmen while voodoo and witchcraft are used to conjure up or disperse evil spirits in other communities.

Even as society begins to accept that the mentally handi-capped are not part of the mentally deranged groups there remains an inbuilt fear of those afflicted even though many of them are the most delightful characters.

In the last two thousand years Christian teachings have followed Bible quotations calling for those possessed of demons to be put to death. During the Middle Ages many thousands of 'mentally ill' people were horribly put to death in the name of religion with a misguided fervour which must have been fuelled by fear. Is it any wonder that even in this supposedly enlightened age many sufferers will go to inordinate lengths to avoid the mental illness tag which still carries with it the dreadful stigma.

So the basic question becomes, how much of an individual's actions are really by choice? Whilst medical science has demonstrated that what enters the body internally in food, drink and medicines affects the way people behave, they have not yet identified external factors which may drive his actions. With so many differing things from genes to gravity affecting emotions, obsessions and compulsions can anyone claim to be really free? There are millions of people living in every part of the world who would gladly sacrifice their supposed freedom for the ability to enjoy those things which they dream of as normal, such as good health and freedom from fear.

During the latter part of the twentieth century there has been a growing increase in the number of studies going on around the globe on how environmental changes brought about by Man himself are affecting his health. Groups seeking political changes have used the tactics of scaremongering towards achieving their ends and have clouded much of the useful work which the scientific community has done. Members of this world, other than those whose main preoccupation is survival, have time to consider future problems but are confused by claim and counter claim and cannot distinguish whether the information they are being given has been adjusted to bend the truth, suppressed to avoid embarrassment, panic, or responsibility, or provided to blur the real truth. It is past time that the human race were given honest-to-goodness balance of probability appraisals on which to judge the needs of their world. Changes may take years, or tens of years, to achieve but with the growing threat to his world Man must take immediate action to reverse the decline.

This can only be done on a world-wide basis with Man acting with Man, for the poor cannot be expected to grow poorer while not using the natural resources of their countries to get money to feed them. The richer countries, indeed the richer people, must compensate them in order to preserve the world. The prize is, after all, life itself. Man must also seek ways of living which are less destructive to his environment. He should look towards that one great power, the greatest in the universe, that seems to the unitiated relatively untapped but which is so powerful that it exercises complete control of all the bodies in the heavens. Such a power must have an affect upon the actions of Man himself, his total health and life. This power is gravity or the magnetic force fields which dictate the movements, actions and relationships of every star, planet, asteroid and comet in the universe. The power, though invisible, presents effects which Man can see in minor ways such as the tides of the earth's oceans ebbing and flowing twice a day due to the attraction of the moon (and the sun).

From the earliest times recognition of the effect of gravitational fields are shown in the interest in astrological predictions which, when given by a true clairvoyant can, sometimes quite frighteningly, take place as predicted. As with other areas of human knowledge that cannot, within our present limits, be scientifically proven, charlatans have exploited the art and thus hidden the few really gifted artists. They themselves find that their powers cannot work for all people. For some, such an admission casts doubts upon their abilities and rather than

96

admit it they too prostitute their art with further consequential loss of faith both in them and the art itself. But many key figures in history have relied upon astrologers and many continue to do so today. History shows many cases where some people were unable to go against that advice. Were they free?

Add to all those interferences of the mind the normal pressures of society which demands, and receives, conformity of behaviour. Fashion is one example. Another is in the sphere of influence where the views of individuals, or of people collectively grouped, are moulded by what has been dubbed, with a derogatory flavour, the media. It is sometimes said that individuals cannot be influenced by those privileged to reach millions of readers, listeners and viewers, who may present stories in unbalanced attacks, sometimes using only suggestion and innuendo, sometimes arguing that it was a dramatic play and not a true story. But those who are personally affected by such presentations could have their lives devastated when readers, listeners and viewers are led to believe what they read, heard or saw was true. Mud always sticks. But such adjusted or incorrect truths affect everyone as they also undermine the social structure in which they live. It is said that every individual is free to choose what he believes but where does he derive the facts on which to base his views in the first place?

On a more mundane level is the inability of the vast majority to ignore what their neighbours think. Keeping up appearances or competing in displayable items is often compulsive. It is a trait of human nature to envy materialistic treasures while trying to be envied themselves. So their lives are spent firstly at schools, colleges and universities to achieve a knowledgeable base on which to develop a career that brings rewards so that they too may store up material things. Many materialists will drop out of the educational convention in order to earn money to indulge their desires. It can take some years for those persisting with education to catch up and then overtake their contemporaries in the materialistic race. And with another of Man's uncontrollable facets they will divide into different social classes, and with new friends to keep up with they become enclosed in their hierarchical structures flaunting their assumed importance in life by a display of materialistic wealth. In animals it is the pecking order, the first place held by the most powerful. In Man wealth is power. For those who exist in under-developed countries with survival as their main object in life, their society follows the pattern that they have many children so that sufficient may survive to help them in their old age.

Either way conformity is all.

When looking at freedom of action those studying investigative interviewing are aware that what the interviewer says and does, and how he says and does it, both controls and rewards the answers he will get. When interviewing suspects of crime for example, if the questioners start with the view that they are speaking to guilty persons their questions and actions will be framed to confirm that view. In interviews it is quite usual for the person being interviewed to try to work out what the questioner wants to hear and to give it to him in order to impress him as a co-operative and competent person. Children and childlike adults are particularly eager to please. Thus leading questions can get misleading answers and the truth becomes distorted. This is not deliberate, this is life.

Even single words can goad individuals into acts which could cost them their lives, let alone their liberty. Chicken, coward, scared, or a simple huh! are examples. Do not believe that many of those goaded into destructive actions had a choice.

The time is well overdue for the term *freedom* to be more closely defined or better understood. Does it mean individuals can go where they like? No. They may go where permitted or, in the case of the vulnerable, only those places where they can feel secure. Does it mean a young lad can climb a tree in the park? No. It is forbidden. Does it mean that individuals can do what they like on their own land such as extend their homes or chop down trees? No. They may need permission to do both. So even general freedom, lauded and defended by many activists, is constrained.

A key question then arises. If members of the human race are carrying out actions which have unknowingly been placed into their minds by internal or external sources and are not objecting to doing so, even arguing that they are doing so by their own free will, can they really be said to be free? Are all those with phobias or those cunningly pushing themselves unchecked towards death freely choosing to be that way? Many people are driven by compulsions and no-one can be certain that they are always aware of it and if they are not, are they considered to be free?

The use of chemicals, or machinery which may change the electrical balance in local environments, may affect some part of the atmosphere around earth which in turn could be affecting Man's health, physical or mental, without him knowing. Would this be freedom? Does anyone really know how much of individual's actions are decided by themselves and not driven, say by inherited traits? Take it a stage further. If humanity were to discover a method of controlling individual's actions without them being aware of it such that they all worked together with a common aim for all peoples of the world with no wars, no killing, no hunger or thirst, could that be defined as freedom? Man has a terrible fear of such a freedom which is so often graphically displayed in films and television stories. Such actions are always seen as dehumanizing the population: and better death than enforced freedom and pleasure.

In these circumstances can freedom be defined as each individual doing what he thinks he wishes to do, provided his actions do not interfere with those of other inhabitants of the planet? Such a definition would be alien to many people and the use of emotive terms like brain-washing would be enough to ensure its sterility by fear. How many people would reject this concept of freedom because they feel that there are too many evil people in the world who would seek a way to exploit the process? For throughout the world one individual cannot trust another.

Trust comes only with truth. If total trust could be achieved on this world by sacrificing Man's supposed freedom to the truth would he be prepared to make it? For without truth there is no hope, and without hope there is no future for Mankind.

8

Tolerance is the antipathy of freedom.

Over the years the people of the world have gradually come to tolerate terrible evils, with their elected representatives doing nothing except give advice on how to avoid them. For our part we do little more for our children, making them withdraw into a limited world of mistrust, and fear of all people, stranger and friend alike. Over the twentieth century many countries abandoned the penalty of death feeling that its retention made their societies as barbaric as the killers themselves. But the thought behind that attitude, which has held sway against the tide, highlights the crux of the problems facing the world today, for in the good versus evil battle only one side is playing by the rules and that side cannot win.

Both the lawful and the unlawful see the clear reluctance to act. This encourages the latter to threaten greater violence and death and the former to strongly believe they cannot be protected against those threats and act accordingly. More and greater violence is fuelled by the success of the unlawful and by the growing fear and the consequential justified lack of confidence which the lawful have in their protectors.

And so, round the world in the 1990s two types of terror reign relatively free, cutting across everyone's lives, yet such is the power of good that only defensive measures, such as increasing security precautions, are actioned, which do nothing to combat the problem. In the not too distant future unless the evil is first contained and then destroyed, the power of good will be self-defeated resulting in catastrophic violence which will, by necessity, be far greater than the way of evil itself.

The two forms of evil are directly related but affect peoples lives in different ways. The first, from which the second is feeding, is terrorism. In the 1980s the developed nations eventually learned the lesson of the futility of war although they continued to encourage them in poorer nations by manipulating them in the horrific game of power politics. But around the world fanatical minority groups discovered terrorism, a more insidious replacement for war which does require a balance of forces. Thus even tiny minorities could hold the vast majority to ransom. Sometimes their objective would be to seize power and use extreme fear, blackmail and murder to maintain it. At other times it is simply an all-consuming hatred which drives them to their insane acts. But throughout the world there are governments who, with the tacit approval of their people, openly encourage this insanity. Indeed some actually carry out training in that horrific trade supplying the life-taking tools to any organization whose business is terror.

And when it comes to hate a frightening number of acts of terror are carried out each year under the banners of religion and politics. Sadly in many countries they have become the twin malignancies of Man's sanity, driving him ever deeper into the pit of inhumanity. The contagion of hatred has been allowed to burgeon, bringing insanity with whole nations embroiled in stupid, genocidal civil wars. In all cases death, maiming and destruction are the menus from which the terrorists feed, initially to force their opinions on others. Hatred prevents compromise.

The terrorist code is simple; select soft targets, that is those where there is little or no risk to themselves, and indiscriminately kill or injure anyone not supportive of their cause. It is part of their creed to proudly declare their responsibility for their inhuman crimes, publicly claiming that dispensing horror advances their cause. But all too often it develops into a crying need to satiate that uncontrollable hatred which burns in their hearts. Men, women, children and babies are sacrificed in their impelled need to satisfy inhuman blood lusts. For most active terrorist killers the cause has long since taken second place.

And far from being ostracized by the societies in which these barbaric killers live, their crimes not only go unpunished but they are protected, even lauded, by individuals, groups and even more regrettably, by nations themselves. The instruments of death – arms, ammunition and explosives – are freely available from those nations willing to spread terror, from those people who are prepared to make money at the expense of other's misery, or from those politically opposed to the government of the country. The tragedy is that previously peaceful people get vortexed by the hatred that terror unleashes and, by providing money and moral support to their selected bunch of killers, they become as guilty of the heinous crimes as their representatives who carry them out.

They exult in a death brought about by those they support and they fling hatred and invective to those caught in between factions and trying to maintain some semblance of order for the people who have to live with it. Attempted justification of such horrors by supposedly civilized people under the euphemism of freedom fighters or guerrillas is inexcusable and wrong. There is no justification whatever for this utterly cowardly, no-risk way of killing and spreading fear, and individual nations must be made to face up to their responsibilities by disgorging those within their borders who feed on death. The problem can be tackled and beaten when the nations, particularly the powerful nations, decide it must end.

But politics over-rides sanity.

One of Man's common failings is his inability to give credit for intelligence to other people around him in his daily circle. In politics this fault is magnified until many leaders achieve megalomania, becoming certain that they are always right and skilfully, or in some cases murderously, remove anyone who disagrees with them. For they become convinced their politics are perfect and a threat to them becomes a threat to their leadership. Many nations have recognized this destructive fault and have prescribed limits to the terms of their elected Leader to prevent it. And so, in the ways of politics, blind eyes are shown to those giving moral or financial support to killers, unless of course such support were for an opposing political regime. Deaf ears are turned to the pitiful cries of anguish from the human life degradingly sucked into power politics.

Sanity can only return when those governments and their people who deal in death and provide succour to terrorists become aware that there is a price to pay and that price is extremely high.

Throughout the world tragedy and violence is encouraged in two distinct ways. Firstly by governments themselves providing finance, arms and ammunition to rebel groups because they are opposed to the politics of the country. Secondly by doing nothing within their own borders to stop fund-raising

102

activities for instruments of death. Thus no government is blameless for the failure of the world to curb terrorism. Indeed their actions lend respectability to those warped inhuman killers who are personally engaged in inflicting death. Screams enough to waken the dead are raised by terrorist supporters, and politicians looking desperately for anything to criticize, when those who have killed without compunction and with scant regard for human life, are on the receiving end of death themselves. It is considered unfair, immoral and illegal for those whose job it is to uphold the law to use subterfuge or lies to obtain the truth and heavy punishment is given to anyone who even suggests working to the same rules as the killers.

This demonstration of Man's ineffectiveness to curb terrorism has had a knock-on effect on individuals throughout the world. The depth to which they are affected depends, to a large extent, upon their own personal involvement in the tragedies caused by the terror. The vast majority of people do not witness the anguish first hand and their main reaction is anger and revulsion at the acts carried out by fellow humans. That anger, which dissipates in a short time, is aimed at the organizations responsible for the violence as well as against those who overtly support such killers. But it becomes an immense personal disaster when individuals or their families are directly involved in the horrors themselves. But even for those not personally involved, bombs in streets, public places or projected at specific soft targets; hi-jacking and planting bombs on planes; and other indiscriminate methods of slaughter, bring a dreadful fear hovering overhead, producing tremendous stress and bursts of panic at any unusual noise or disturbance. If this fear is not contained it will consume those who have to live their daily lives in a community ruled by fear and will inevitably result in the backlash of a strike-first mentality.

The lack of purpose within governments to deal with terrorism has produced reflective images in societies where aggressive and violent behaviour on the streets exposes a similar lack of purpose. Laws are written with inadequate police powers which lends further encouragement to individuals and smaller groups to violence and terror of a more general kind.

Many millions of people can normally distance themselves from the pain inflicted by the horrors of religious or political terrorism which lie elsewhere. But the ghosts of local killers lurk silently in every city street, in every country lane, on trains, roads, in lifts and dark alleys, car parks, within homes, indeed anywhere, waiting, it seems to many, to vent their demands on the unprotected. In the same cowardly way as the terrorist they select easy soft targets.

The local killer, rapist or crook attacks the vulnerable, less protected, weaker members of society, which means women, children and the elderly. There seems to be no limit to the depths of depravity to which they will sink. What is it which drives them to such abhorrent actions? Are you really convinced that it is not possible that their violent driving emotion can be over-ridden by a stronger emotion, such as the fear of the death penalty? Why does society continue to limit the punishment of those individuals who, for example, have raped, robbed and killed a harmless old lady, or who have viciously sexually assaulted a child, perhaps tying them up to be thrown away to die a lingering and painful death? Or for those individuals who have battered harmless, feeble people to death for no apparent motive? By what rules of behaviour do the killers play? Are we right in allowing such insane wickedness to be treated with kindness and consideration? And can anyone really claim that such kindness will halt the continuing growth of such terror?

Revenge demands death. But that is classed by many as a barbaric and an unacceptable passion in civilized circles, and conditioned thinking says it must not be allowed. But why should those who wish to vent their anger upon anyone who has totally destroyed their lives be made to feel guilty about their feelings? Is it that syndrome again, that to give way to emotions, compulsions or anything else which drives them, is considered weak by society and thus unacceptable? What sort of society is it where cold blooded killers see no threat to themselves except, at most, risking a few years in jail?

If anything is barbaric surely it is the death and the manner of death of innocent victims. When applied to the super inhuman tragedy of the killing of a baby it becomes obscene. Moralists argue that death of any sort is barbaric, but with only one side playing to the rules the inevitable consequences are a loss of confidence in the protecting agencies and a threatening fear which curtails the freedom of those who see themselves as unprotected. The absence of the penalty of death also seems to many that murder, added to other crimes such as rape and robbery with violence, goes virtually unpunished. If prospective killers knew, *without doubt*, that the consequences of their actions were the death penalty, would not those who defy that law and kill people who are unknown to them, for any reasons, including those in the (depending on whose side one is on) currently 'justifiable' vogue of political crimes, abdicate their right to life? Surely we must accept that a firm penalty of death would save, at the very least, some victims? Or is it possible that, in moments of calmer thought not driven by fierce emotions, tucked away in the deep recesses of the human mind is the knowledge that such acts are not committed voluntarily and in those circumstances to demand a life in return would be barbaric?

It is said that most murders are committed within families for a variety of reasons. Probably because everyone has some understanding of how passions can push some people beyond their control to injure or kill, and because they are not indiscriminate in their selection of victims, the cry for vengeance is muted to the families involved. Many can see how the penalty of death may be inappropriate in such cases.

In all discussions on the death penalty the strongest argument, which over-rides all others, is that the penalty of death leaves no room for errors, and they do occur.

To many lay people the law between nations, and within them, seems better able to cope with those criminals who have stolen material wealth from their fellow man rather than in dealing with killers. National borders can, and do, offer havens to killers. Politicians of all parties avoid publicly supporting calls for the death penalty because such actions may be unpopular with many august and powerful members of society. Others live in a cloistered, moralistic world believing there is no valid reason whatever for killing another human being regardless of the absolute certainty that, given the opportunity, the killer will strike again. Turning the other cheek can only be acceptable if it is their own cheek and not those of the vulnerable members of their society. Some people can even wallow in a glut of self righteous forgiveness as long as they are not personally involved in the pain and suffering.

War is different. Animals are different. And avoidance

results in inactivity.

Such procrastination takes no account of any rights the vulnerable have to be protected, particularly the old and those living on their own, who become imprisoned in their homes with fear. For many years now most elderly people have been frightened to answer their door and are unable to venture out unless they are certain they can be back when there are plenty of people about. Rarely, and then only in an emergency, do they feel they can venture out alone after dark. As it has become clear to the criminals that it is not possible to harden soft targets and that, if caught, they face outdated inadequate punishments, crimes of violence have grown in their ferocity and their audacity. Such acts have shown how protective legislation and processes are inadequate and have simply been an encouragement to others to indulge in their own violent activities.

So today, children and women who go about their normal tasks alone cannot move freely. Their sub-conscious minds have to be trained to carry out a continuous sweep of their surroundings, like radar, maintaining a constant awareness of what is going on. They must also unconsciously be thinking ahead about where they are going. They must try to ensure where possible that there are several solid looking citizens or someone in uniform, preferably a policemen, within view. They must avoid, at all costs, placing themselves in a position where they would be alone and thus become a soft target. They cannot take short cuts, to the contrary they often have to make long detours to avoid lonely or unlit paths. They are unable, without fear, to walk their dogs even during the day in those places where the animals should be taken to mess, which is away from the areas laid down for the local people, such as recreation grounds.

As their normal every day actions involve some risk, however slight, the vulnerable live fearful lives. Statistics are used to show the rarity of attacks and to try and offer some comfort to those wrestling with such fears. But an attacker can strike anywhere at any time and there are no statistics to show the fear that accompanies those who venture out feeling so helplessly alone. For them simple actions like collecting cars from car parks can become a hurdle of fear both by day and night. Even having gained the comparative safety of their cars their worries are not over. The 'radar sweep' must be boosted by consciously looking to see that the car is empty and that they are not being followed home or down any quiet roads they may have to take on their journey. Such has become our acceptance of these horrific attacks that the phrase 'well, she was asking for trouble' is unkindly and unjustifiably said about many who may have had a temporary lapse in their concentration or may, by circumstances, have been forced to abandon their normal code of not being out alone after dark.

For despite all their precautions the vulnerable can find themselves on occasions placed in extremely frightening positions where the risk heightens. To whom do they turn? How long does it take before all those who are concerned for their safety are branded paranoid? But is there anyone who is not having difficulty suppressing their fears for the safety of their vulnerable loved ones? The severe stress which people at risk have to undergo until they recover the position can be traumatic and linger in their minds for a long time. The society in which they live generally discourages fearful people from seeking help from the nearest source and that regrettably increases the risk of attack.

And yet it is only a few years ago that the parents of today's school children themselves went to school and were able to walk alone down unlit lanes without fear of attack. An offer of a lift was often gratefully accepted. In today's world lifts are rarely offered or accepted and even those who seek them are shunned by most drivers who are themselves fearful of the risk of attack. Wherever an attacker secretly selects to lurk becomes unsafe for the vulnerable. There is even danger to children as they play in their own street or pop to the local shops. Statistics do nothing to stem the fear of parents that, during a lapse of their vigilance, their own child may be abducted, sexually assaulted or murdered. Their freedom, and those of their children, are curtailed as everyday living has to be adapted around restrictive rules which have to be made simply to avoid making them vulnerable to a possible attacker, or to avoid the distressing, gut wrenching over-reaction because a loved one is later than normal.

Ladies are particularly vulnerable. They cannot feel safe while travelling or when their business requires them to meet strangers. Each abduction brings in its wake more fear and less freedom. Their 'normal' lives are adjusted until restrictions become everyday matters and thus not noticeable, tolerated by an unaware society. For new generations the maxim that you don't miss what you have never had is apposite for 'freedom', and shows that it is relative. Individuals have to adopt their own codes of practice. It may be the railway season ticket holders who take a taxi over the route of their normal train journey to avoid travelling on trains late in the evening. But even taxis are risky. However the vulnerable travel, the risk of attack is low, say the statistics, but victims of abduction, rape and murder are indiscriminate and statistics cannot calm the fearful.

Travelling by car also has its risk particularly when unscheduled stops occurs such as a breakdown. Lone lady drivers get no relief from fear knowing that most law-abiding men will drive past even though they desperately want to help, because they too know the risk she is running simply by being on her own. Each man would hope that, should his own wife or children get into a similar situation that some kindly, helpful person would not leave them stranded, alone and open to attack. But they are afraid that their offer of help would be misunderstood and panic the already fearful lady, and they would probably be right. So they drive on, justifying their actions to themselves but embarrassed by the feelings which make them turn away from helpless individuals. The pain, anger, doubts and recrimination tears a gaping hole in the lives of those caring people who passed by when they hear that a woman had disappeared from that spot. What can they say to the family of the missing woman? What can they say to themselves? What can society say to either? Why should they have to go through the trauma of deep guilt anyway when, as individuals, they are blameless?

Even children arrogantly defy authority with little fear of retribution. They are aware that they can no longer be chastised by a cuff round the ear and society will roundly condemn any that try. And with the lack of punishment their confidence grows as they expand to graffiti and the destruction of property. Any witnesses know that to speak out could make them and, worse, their families a target for attack, so they remain silent and shrug off such events as other's problems. It is impossible to criticize their actions in a world where protection is denied but it is thus that the offences are compounded and vandals, hooligans and criminals are born.

So what has happened to the freedom of the lawful individual? Are these the liberties so fiercely defended by activists? Is it right that only the physically strong or those who can afford to buy muscle are free from fear? Those in government must be fearful for their own lives but no soft target they. How is it possible that they, or indeed the people themselves, are allowing a tiny few to rule the lives of many millions, contrary to their wishes? As this century moves towards its close it is fashionable for those not poverty stricken or fearful to talk and write about human rights, but who are the protagonists for the rights of the vulnerable people, those oppressed and imprisoned by fear of attacks whether real or imagined? Are not ordinary everyday folk entitled to protection? Wars have been fought for less.

One organization after another has looked for the reasons for the growth in violence and sadly politicians have abused their powers by encouraging, or refusing to discourage it in their endeavours to make political gains. So the truth is shrouded.

One area in which so much has been said or written is the teaching standards at schools, yet rarely mentioned is the disruption of lessons by bad behaviour. Why? It has become endemic in classrooms with both teachers and pupils accepting it as the norm, only being noticed when it spills over its usual boundaries. Probably unaware of what actually goes on in schools, parents expect teachers to control such disruptions, which may very likely be by the same individuals which they themselves had, by their own silence, allowed to desecrate their village. So our tolerance of bad behaviour is demonstrated to our schoolchildren who may have the whole of their future lives affected by a very tiny minority, those few making teachers' jobs much more difficult and stressful. Children notice the helplessness of those in charge to deal effectively with disruptive elements and some can be encouraged or dared into similar actions.

Teachers cannot be blamed, society can. So, by its inactivity, society breeds the vandal and violent criminal of the future. Does society not, at the very least, owe it to those youngsters who want to do well at school by giving them the peace to concentrate on their studies? Disruptions will particularly affect those subjects which individual children find difficult. Once behind they can lose the subject altogether. Teachers are entrusted with shaping the lives of future generations; why then are they denied the use of punishments which only they, as the person in charge, may decide are necessary to stop disruptions?

Is it not time we began to face the real facts of life? If the price of protection for the vulnerable members of the community can only be paid at the expense of some loss of liberty, can society deny that price? How much longer, how many more lives must be shattered, how many more deaths must occur before the world recognizes the size of the problem? Trust is rapidly being dissolved in the mists of fear. The violent now openly and arrogantly rule many areas of a town or city. Since they seem untouchable, since they can carry on their activities seemingly unheeded, the people have become afraid to speak out for, with such apparent flouting of the law, they fully believe that they cannot be protected. And in its wake develops the philosophy of the three monkeys, hear no evil, see no evil, speak no evil, and with it the proportionate growth in violence and aggression.

To many the fear surrounding their lives day and night throughout the year is so real that they are forced out of the area in which they were born, that is those who are able to move. There are a growing number of drawbridges being raised by individuals who, to reduce their fears to a containable level, are isolating themselves from the reality of what is occurring around them. They have been driven by fear to helplessly watch violence taking place and do nothing, not even provide information against the culprits How many millions of people have perforce already raised the drawbridge on life?

Yet more stress is caused by the anarchistic effect that has unknowingly been caused by many usually kind and considerate people whilst seeking publicity for their own political or moral objectives. Police forces have become the target to attack either physically by missile throwing (sometimes with bottles full of human excreta), by selective criticisms and by underhand innuendo, often full of half-truths which make them so difficult to refute. The verbal attacks have been vociferous and have come from many eminent people. Yet most of the criticisms are wrongly aimed at the law enforcers and should be redirected to the law-makers. Such attacks have had two serious consequences for the freedom of Man. Firstly they have cast doubts on the integrity of police forces, thus undermining their authority to deal effectively with law breakers and bring louder calls to curb their powers. Secondly they have diverted large police resources away from their prime task, the protection of the population. Thus many well-meaning people have, by their actions, brought increased fear to the vulnerable in the communities.

Sometimes the laws themselves are declared political by those opposed to them and the police are pilloried as supporters of those politics. But laws are made in the legislative assemblies in which, in democracies, both government and opposition parties have had their input. Police are required to uphold all laws regardless of their own personal opinions. One might as well blame the soldiers, sailors and airmen for the wars in which they fought and died.

The sad part is that churchmen and politicians have either openly supported and praised those engaged in attacks against the police or in other violent disorders, or have seemed by their lack of condemnation to have silently done so. Many have seized every opportunity they can to isolate, out of context, those events critical of the police and support criticisms with arguments similar to those used by terrorist killers. So, perhaps for the first time, national leaders have, by such actions, been advocating that individuals can be selective about which laws they should obey. Such is the spring of anarchy. It is a tragedy to the whole human race that such an august body as the Anglican Church passed a resolution at its conference in 1988 accepting, for ungodly internal political reasons, that violence becomes acceptable when all else fails to achieve justice.

Surely it should be the duty of all politicians and churchmen to condemn violence in any form and not promote selectivity of laws to seek political gain or to maintain cohesion amongst their members at the ultimate expense of those they claim to represent. When does the price become too high to pay?

When it comes to punishment there cannot be many things more barbaric and degrading than incarceration. Those who have not experienced prison life have to form judgements on it from the differing and sketchy pictures that are published from time to time and they too can bend the truth for political or monetary gain. There is, however, little doubt that people are conditioned by their environment. The soldier who goes to war and is involved in action gets conditioned to kill (which tragically can sometimes run over into civilian life when the war is over). People who move house change and become typical of the area in which they live and the type of house they live in. Similarly, prison inmates spend all their prison time in a criminal club atmosphere where their standing in life may be measured by their violent nature. Such environments breed problems rather than solving them. Because of the inmates' common interest prisons are often referred to as the universities of crime.

Certainly, criminals learn new crafts or develop new criminal deals as well as getting to know each other well enough to assess their individual skills and potential for use in future crimes. Does anyone really believe that prison leads to rehabilitation for the violent criminal?

The actions of all individuals on earth are affected by, amongst other things, the society which surrounds them. Thus one result of failing to provide justice is more crime.

But questions have long remained unanswered regarding how much control people have over their urges or their need to satiate their thirst for excitement by turning to crime. Can anyone be absolutely certain that, in some cases like the smoker who cannot stop, the criminals may not be able to curb their behaviour? In which case does this make incarceration simply a tool to remove the problem from the public arena and thus reduce the dreadful fears of those directly involved?

Certainly the present laws do provide for those individuals who have committed crimes of violence but have been medically declared not mentally responsible. The law says they should not be punished but simply locked away to remove the problem from the public arena. But if we recognize that individuals can be moved by powerful drives and may not be able to resist them, is punishment the right answer? Man has always used it as a deterrent to crime but it can only really deter by making fear over-ride other driving emotions. Many can have their dominant emotion controlled by a real threat to them as individuals so that, even with minds as complex as the human, the general levels of punishment can be adequate to deter them. But they will only work if the risk of being caught is high and they can be applied swiftly. Otherwise there is no threat.

But they are inadequate to deter hardened, compelled criminals and it becomes necessary to find out if there are any punishments which would worry them enough personally to over-ride their criminal emotions. But in doing so Man must guard against his own need for revenge to be satisfied. Lord Hewart's famous statement is as relevant today as it was when he made it in 1923.

'It is not merely of some importance but is of fundamental importance that justice should not only be done, but should manifestly and undoubtedly be seen to be done.'

Sadly we do not see justice done today. And if we are determined to eradicate crime why have we not only removed the instant justice of beating or corporal punishment but actually prosecute those who use it?

How long can the situation continue to deteriorate for the aged, for children, for women, before a backlash of vigilantes try to do what they see governments failing to do? There have been signs of such frustration boiling over in the behaviour of a very few ill-advised police officers. Such action only makes matters worse and must be rooted out, roundly condemned and punished. But the message signs must be heeded, for if vigilantes do arise then so will chaos, horror and barbarism reign unchecked. No sensible person wants that to happen.

The acceptable trends of societies can often be seen through the heroes which they adopt. The new heroes, like their predecessors, generally show good triumphing over evil, but they demonstrate two very disturbing differences. Firstly, unlike earlier heroes they do not hand over the crooks to the sheriff or other forces of law and order. Secondly they clearly demonstrate how the latter's powers have been curbed so that they now have an inability to act. Thus the hero, with the law-enforcer looking the other way and making it appear totally justifiable, and indeed necessary if justice is to be done, appoints himself judge, jury and executioner. He dispenses destruction, violence and death to the great satisfaction of most people. Concerned governments, who can see the dangers of this satisfaction growing through approval to acclaim, are looking for ways to stop, before they start, presentations which encourage such ideas. But the presentations are only showing what is seething in people's minds. It is there in films, on television, in stories and people have welcomed it with enthusiasm.

Each one of the thousands of millions of people on this planet is an individual who understands his own feelings and is conditioned by his society (and perhaps his ancestors and other unknown forces beyond his control) to distinguish right from wrong. He compares what he considers to be his own iron self-control to the ways others act, branding those who do not meet his self-imposed standards as weak, and those that do better as unnecessarily strict, or even stupid. Few, if any, are honest about the way they feel and act, keeping secret those ideas or practices which they feel demonstrate weaknesses. Failure to control actions is seen as a weakness on their part, and they thus hide their problems, putting forward the face which they feel those around them want to see. People who spend all their lives together do not know whether their partners are compelled to actions of which they are ashamed, yet in a fascination of horror enjoy. Until compulsion is understood partners will keep their secrets. Life is an act.

For many years it has often been said of those who commit crimes of murder that they were 'not right in the head'. When a crime revolts people to their stomachs they can think of no more condemning statement than 'he must be sick'. And the world is learning fast that many individuals of the human race act, deliberately and with cunning, knowingly but helplessly, to their own detriment. In the same way people can act, under the influence of the same power, to the detriment of other people. No one wants to accept this because to do so would be seen as an encouragement to those hovering on the fringe and able, perhaps with difficulty, to control their actions.

All individuals are as different as their finger prints each having their own irresistible impulses or urges with varying degrees of control. Compulsion does not permit decisions. Some people are forced to actions despite themselves. They are not weak, they just cannot stop what they are doing and those who can must understand and accept that. Even superstition falls into this area. How many truly superstitious people could continuously flout their obsessions? Without providing alterna-

114

tive ways of controlling the problems there are great difficulties in accepting, privately or publicly, the view that individuals are unable to prevent their actions, for to do so would undoubtedly encourage people to indulge their needs with no guilt, regret or concern. It would also encourage liars and cheats to exploit such tolerant understanding. Thus, at present, there seems no alternative but to keep punishing those unable, or possibly unwilling, to follow the laws.

The level of punishment however must be justified by its objectives. Is it to deter further similar crimes or, God forbid, to seek revenge for a crime done? What punishment will deter if the compulsive drive of the criminal remains dominant at the end of his term in prison? Is it fair either to society or the ex-prisoners themselves to release such personalities to carry out the same crime again? If we cannot legislate to protect the vulnerable against attack can we provide them with a visual warning of possible danger? In bygone days criminals were branded so that they could be spotted wherever they went. Barbaric but effective. Some countries have adopted a tagging system which enables them to track where an individual is at any time. It actually give offenders greater freedom by not requiring them to report to the authorities so regularly. At the same time the tag is a watchdog and its presence is a deterrent.

There exists a case of extending the tagging system to anyone who has been guilty of attacking the vulnerable. But in our protection of criminal's rights we have laws to expunge past crimes from the records after a certain time. There are also laws to forbid placing the past criminal records before those who are required to decide guilt or innocence. For some reason we will retreat from tagging as we will from colour-tagging which would identify the crime which had been committed. But such tagged people would immediately be recognized by the public, the police, managers of restaurants and drinking establishments, thus allowing preventative measures to be taken. Persistent trouble makers could be tagged so that they could be excluded from bunching together and causing hooli-ganism. Tagged people could also be prevented from leaving their own country without the specific approval of the courts. Why should it be wrong for communities to know if persistent trouble is wandering in their locale? Arguments that such punishment would be inhumane raises the question of whether it would deter, because if it did, it would be more inhumane to the fearful, law-abiding majority not to do so.

Before any punishment can be given guilt must be established. This is not easy when the laws have been designed over centuries to ensure the protection of the innocent. But so much emphasis has been placed on this that the law is now overprotecting the guilty and thus failing in its prime role of protecting the innocent from the criminal. Justice has become a game and not an end. Esoteric arguments abound on the meanings of the words used in the laws and, in far too many cases, whether a person is guilty of a crime or not has become irrelevant. Lord Hewart's words ring hollow today. What has become more important in justice is whether the police and law officers followed the proper procedures in bringing the charge, whether witnesses can be discredited or whether trickery was used to gain the truth. Justice has thus become a mockery and has further heightened public fears and mistrust. There is a growing feeling that the police are refusing to deal with people's legitimate reports of crime and they cannot understand that without evidence in the form required by the courts, it is the prosecutors not the police who decide not to proceed with the case, leaving the latter to explain to the victims. The blame for the lack of protection falls on them and they are condemned as incompetent and trust in them is further eroded. As trust diminishes, fear increases.

And we can all see how justice is done as we see thousands of cases dismissed every year by the courts on technicalities, regardless of the guilt of the accused. A typical case was where police were questioning an individual who they suspected of petrol bombing a car but the allegation was denied. He was of course protected under the law which says he is not obliged to say anything. It was explained to the individual that a fingerprint had been found on a fragment of glass from the bottle whereupon a full confession was given. In the court it came out that the fingerprint did not exist and it had merely been a subterfuge to gain the truth. The judge dismissed the case because the confession was not fairly obtained. That is what we have come to accept as justice.

And what about justice on self-defence, once assumed to be a God-given right? Individuals, and there may be more than one, can break into your house, or mine, under the protection of a law which only allows occupants to use reasonable force against intruders. To make matters worse the latter is judged by people well after the event. How can anyone be expected to know how a person felt at the time? Those breaking in would, by pre-planning, know exactly the risks they would be taking. The occupants on the other hand may have wakened from their sleep or found the intruder on entering their house and would have no idea what the intruders' objectives were. Every individual would react differently so that, even if those judging had experienced a similar entry into their homes, it would not be possible for them to grasp the extent of the terror which drove the defensive actions. But why should innocent people have to justify their actions against intruders who were there ostensibly of their own free will? Thus the law does not permit people to properly protect themselves against others who have entered their home illegally and may be bent on murder, rape, other violence or robbery. If occupants were to install devices inside their property which could inflict injury or death on those illegally entering they would be charged and punished through the courts.

Why? Is this justice? Intruders have no such inhibitions or rules. Burglaries are often more costly to investigate than the items stolen and, unless there is a good chance of a conviction, takes a low, often nil, priority in the allocation of police resources. But it takes many victims a number of years to overcome the trauma of having their homes invaded and seeing their belongings and personal things desecrated by an un-known, uninvited hand. For if their own home is not safe, is anywhere? The metaphoric shrug at the police station helps neither victim nor the image of the police. Add to that the victim's fear, built from the knowledge that if it happened once it could happen again, which brings the touch of an icy finger down their spine at every unusual noise, event or even a knock on the door. Sometimes the fear is so great it drives people from their homes to escape from it, or it may drive them to a nervous breakdown which devastates the whole of their future life as well as that of their families. Why is this allowed to happen? Why does society tolerate such heartbreak to its citizens?

Devices could be designed to protect individuals in their homes which could hand out a knock-out blow to any intruder. The argument that it may bring about the possible death of an intruder with a specific health problem is irrelevant. A warning sign could be placed in prominent position so that intruders were fully aware of the risks of their actions. Why is there this reluctance, nay refusal, to allow people, particularly the weaker members of society, to protect themselves? What alternative can the strong offer the weak? How much longer is society going to ignore the real fears of women living on their own, of the elderly, of parents, of children?

It is easier to understand the argument that street protection devices, such as a stun gun which delivers an electric pulse sufficient to paralyse an assailant, could be wrongly used against innocent people simply because the owner used it in fear when they had assumed, incorrectly, that they were about to be attacked. So once more the vulnerable are unprotected and the police will fulfil the law which does not permit such devices to be carried. Users in justified self-defence or even carriers will be prosecuted. If used by the lawless they must first be found and the culprit will only be charged if the evidence will stand a chance of being proven in court. Is this fair to the unprotected? If they cannot protect themselves who can?

There has to be a way of dealing with all these problems which are thrust upon lawful society by a tiny criminal minority. And there is, but it will require a willingness to want a solution. Conditioned thinking must be abandoned, it means nurturing all that is good and cutting out that which is bad; it demands the death of secrecy, calling for an openness and understanding between individuals, friends and foe alike; but above all it calls for the imposition of truth. Such objectives would mean sacrificing many long held prejudices and the end of animal reactive thinking. It would allow those who know they need help to overcome their anti-social behaviour to get help without stigma. And priorities must be decided in world terms so that the poorer nations become the responsibility of the richer.

The way ahead lies in the powerhouse which operates within every individual in the world directing and controlling all feelings and actions. In every human those powerhouses are different. They are constantly subjected to local and cosmic changes which affect the drives of individuals from day to day. And therein lies the way to salvation, for through those powerhouses behaviour can be changed. The knowledge of how to do that is already here but we may allow our fear of change to stop its use. Difficult though it may be the control of those personal powerhouses must, at all costs, be held in the hands of the peaceful and law-abiding members of the human race, and used, or they will be swept away by inactivity against evil.

Such a control will affect individual's way of life and will be seen as an interference, indeed attack against the freedom of the individual. But the benefits it will produce would be beyond measure and bring world peace, abolish fear and bring freedom on a scale unparalleled in human history.

9

The human body is an extremely complex, fully automatic, chemical factory and its operation is what makes the individual feel and act as he does. It takes some understanding but the process has begun. It is known for example, incredible though it may seem and miraculous as it is, that all animal and plant life begins with a single cell which only begins to split and develop when fertilized by the sperm of the opposite sex. Imagine the fantastic complexity of that single cell in Man, as contained within it are the complete instructions for making an adult human being with biologically timed milestones throughout life which, unless those instructions are interrupted in any way, will be carried through to death.

In the human as the cells split the brain begins to build itself by connecting together billions of nerve cells. Those preset biological signals issue instructions at different stages and are instrumental in the brain formation. Two months after conception the foetus looks like a brain and it is at this time at its most vulnerable. The network of nerves and tissues stretch like fibres throughout the now spherical brain and nerve cells or neurons migrate along them each with specific destinations, tasks and timescales. At this crucial time neurons are being produced at the rate of a quarter of a million per minute.

The shape of things to come is dictated by two prominent drivers, inheritance and environment. The brain is particularly vulnerable to the latter between eight and sixteen weeks after conception. It is known, for example, that irradiation and alcohol can disrupt the migration of the brain cells, the former damaging the fibres and stopping them in their tracks; the latter causing the neurons to overshoot their targets. Either way all babies affected are born small and are retarded. Those damaged by the foetal alcohol syndrome can have hyperactivity, compulsiveness, temper tantrums, short memory span, perceptive disorders and be very sensitive with general bad humour. Other factors, such as the mother's diet, are known to be involved in producing similar problems.

It is the brain, using that biological clock gained from the single cell, that signals the initiation of birth. At this time the brain becomes exposed to a flood of new sensory experiences and other inputs which will influence its future growth to double its size by the time the infant reaches seven years of age. And as the brain grows so it sends more messages along its signal lines to make the physical body grow while developing individual attitudes and behaviour patterns. Internal inputs come from the ingestion of food, drink, and breathing, each depending upon the environment of their origin. External inputs are fed to the growing brain through the infant's sensors of sight, hearing, touch, smell and taste. There are other external factors which may affect the brain's development, some yet to be identified. One recognized factor is extra-sensory perception which shows up in the way a baby can detect and react to worry or fear in its number one protector, its mother.

It is said that all babies are born without fear and they only learn it from those around them. The fear which babies detect by extra-sensory perception will deny them the relaxed comfort of not worrying about their own safety and it will be reflected in an uneasy and unhappy child. The doubt which many new mothers display to their children can thus cause a problem until their confidence returns and soothes the baby. Such problems become more difficult if the baby's behaviour, brought on by mother's doubts, causes greater doubt in the mother and gets into a phobic circle. There is insufficient knowledge on other possible environmental factors which may affect baby's growth such as magnetic storms on earth, force fields or noises, both detectable and subliminal or from electrical equipment adjacently sited. There is still a lot awaiting discovery.

Food and drink affects babies in different ways and generally the signs of unsatisfactory feeds are soon made known to the mother. But development can be harmed in a few babies by a food allergy which can, tragically for the families concerned, make them retarded. Other affects of food can clearly be seen in hyperactive children who, given the wrong food or drink,

121

can turn from a well balanced individual into an unreasonable, unhearing, unbearable monster. Food and drink affects people in different ways throughout their lives resulting in a variety of reactions from pleasure through to ecstasy, from despair to suicide, from disease to premature death.

Many unseen particles are ingested through the lungs, probably the most well known in developed countries being from the lead in petrol scattered from car exhausts which can retard growing infants. But insufficient is known about all the effects of environmental pollution brought about by both Man and nature's activities. Dust from the Sahara or other deserts, dust from volcanic activities, dust from anything burned up in earth's atmosphere, dust from accidents like the Chernobyl nuclear disaster, dust from forest fires, dust from burning stubble or other fields, the list is endless. From earth, from sun, from outer space, come more dust particles, all descending to earth to be ingested by Man.

The growing brain is also influenced by nerve impulses through the baby's eyes and ears. If one eye were out of focus for example it would send imperfect information to the brain and the right connections may not be made. Similarly poor hearing gives poor signals. Animal experiments have shown that such abnormalities can injure the brain but it is not yet known whether these results can be read across to the human brain.

Other environmental activities can affect the development of the brain and scaremongering theories with little factual data do little to identify the true causes. The worries of bringing up babies is steeped in old wives tales.

At birth babies have the flexibility to learn any language but by the time they are a year old this fades as they become committed to a single language.

The human moral sense is another milestone which surfaces at about eighteen months which shows itself in the child's concern about a dropped teddy, a broken doll or car, or indeed any toy.

At seven years of age the mind begins to think in the abstract. Up to that age fears were simple: the dark, ghosts, and big dogs, but now change to kidnap, murder, nuclear war or accident.

By this time the brain has about a billion neurons with some ten thousand connections to their neighbours. The brain can now seek new information and learn from its experiences. From that one cell there are now billions of cells all despatched to their proper place unless tragedy has interrupted their journeys.

When fully developed the upper cortex of the brain is divided into two hemispheres which operate mainly independently being linked by nervous tissue. The left hemisphere is the conscious brain and is mainly language orientated with the right covering non-verbal actions. In deep hypnosis the left side of the hemisphere is virtually lost and thus the patient would have difficulty in talking. The relationship between the two hemispheres appears to most people sometime during their lives when they intuitively feel that a speaker to whom they are listening either does not mean what he is saying or is deliberately attempting to deceive his audience. This right brain response can rarely be supported by a satisfactory logical rationale which the left brain requires. The suspicion is created by the verbal left brain statements of the speaker being contradicted by his right brain non-verbal signs. There are many people who class themselves as good judges of character and it is possible that they may have the ability to detect the invisible signs more easily than most.

Many articles have been written about body language but it remains poorly understood how the individual notices the difference between the signs and words and how the message is handled in the conscious mind. Intuition or hunch can drive individuals wild when they feel absolutely certain they are right but are unable to prove it.

With the signal lines developed throughout the body, messages are transmitted to the brain which, in turn, sends its own reactive signals to muscles and glands to protect or stimulate feelings whether of pleasure or displeasure. Thus a cold wind on the skin prompts a message to the brain which arouses the combatants of goose pimples and shivering, to warm the area. Messages through eyes prompt the brain into stimulating a multitude of reactions. Distress, lust, envy, jealousy, greed, hunger, delight, love, indeed all human emotions can be excited through visual contact. The ear too carries its messages, each bringing its own response. The calmness of water lapping on a moored boat or the constant talking of the oceans as the waves break on the shoreline. Music which can lift the spirits or complement those in despair. Rhythm which can excite to exhaustion. A voice which pours love. The other side of the same coin can be where both sight and sound irritate the mind such that even minor events can cause the body's system to be chemically fouled into long moods of unbreakable grumpiness. And in a similar way other signals and brain reactive impulses are started by the other senses of touch, smell and taste.

And most people are aware of their own individual sixth sense and like extra sensory perception this is much more apparent in the mind of children before it closes down into its narrow environment. But Man has a driving need to discover how things fit into his world and his desire to communicate that knowledge to others is overwhelming. Thus all nations continue research in their attempt to discover more about Man himself, his world, and the heavens, all of which affect his life.

As a result of past research he is now aware that a pair of chromosomes are found in every cell in his body, one from the male parent and the other from the female. Chromosomes contain the genes which establish the characteristics of the individual. These hereditary determinants are in the chromosome pairs so they come from either parent. This leads to the view that all attitudes, actions and diseases could be hereditary, the latter lying dormant within the individual waiting for the wrong signal to be nudged into action.

Not all smokers for example get lung cancer and therefore the threat is intangible and inadequate to frighten everybody to stop, or not start, smoking until it is too late. But for those with latent cancer cells smoking stimulates the wrong signal and for them cancer is a certainty. Many related cell/gene structures have been identified within individuals and having started, the excitement created will lead to rapid progress. Indeed lives are already being save by this early warning. Telling someone that cancer is certain if they smoke is a far deadlier and more successful message.

Many people across the world believe their children can be adversely affected by external inputs but are often unable to identify this because the information needed is just beyond the present boundary of knowledge. Studies of the statistical medical cases show that some diseases develop in clusters, suggesting environmental causes. Enter politics. Enter irresponsible reporting. The former use fear whenever possible to make political capital, the latter to sensationalize their news or documentary programme presentations. Such fear is regularly used in the field of nuclear energy. There have been many presentations in picture, sound and print about clusters of leukaemia, particularly in children, being caused by radiation from nearby nuclear stations but few attempt to explain those clusters which exist well away from them. Concerned parents know that irradiation can damage the foetus by interrupting the signal from the brain to the growing body cells thus producing a retarded infant. They are therefore very vulnerable to fear. The problem is that no-one knows what the causes of clusters are. It may be radiation but not necessarily from the plant as the rocks and granite push out radiation in many areas while radioactive gases can form naturally in certain areas. The widest form of radiation spews from the sun, some part of it falling to earth.

It is easy to raise Man's fear of radiation because it cannot be detected by any of his five senses, thus no-one knows when it is presenting a threat. There is no doubt that too much radiation can cause cancer; while that disease itself may be dealt with by the use of radiation. It may or may not be the cause of clusters but there are some indications that they may be due to other causes. Statistical research has shown that many leukaemia clusters occur in new towns where a large part of the population are migrants from many different parts. Other research suggests that leukaemia is one result of improved hygienic conditions and seems to be triggered off in many youngsters who have their first illness later than normal. World studies of differing hygienic conditions seem to support this research. But poor hygiene carries a high infant mortality rate. And still no-one knows how the trigger is pulled. But when knowledge is in short supply the use of fear creates unnecessary worry and stress in many communities.

Where some families have lived in the same area for generations, it is possible they may have unknowingly been close breeding which may have given them a greater share of those inherited latent cells which make them more susceptible than other people to some clustered diseases. Research has shown a clear relationship between many diseases and the hereditary determinants which meant they were built into that first

125

fertilized cell lying dormant until activated. The body usually detects disease intruders, and signals a warning to the brain computer which despatches chemicals to attack the invaders and render them harmless. Sometimes individuals, for a variety of reasons, may not be capable of producing the chemicals necessary to de-activate invading diseases and Man has found medicines to help to prevent and cure many diseases which had been causing a high death rate.

Cancer seems to be one of those diseases which grow without the opposing reactive signals from the brain until it has a good hold, but if a hereditary cell was programmed to become cancerous would the brain detect any need to act?

The number of cases of skin cancer is rising with the malignant variety increasing over the last ten years by an alarming fifty per cent. The sun is the leading cause of skin cancer and the upsurge in cases is blamed partly to the greater number of people exposing themselves to the sun's rays to get a fashionable tan. But ten to twenty miles above the earth's surface lies the ozone layer which absorbs much of the sun's ultraviolet radiation which is harmful to all life. By his free use of chemicals, particularly chlorofluorocarbons, refrigerants and solvents, Man has unknowingly punched a hole in this layer. It is the rays reaching earth through this gap which are blamed by specialists as the major cause of the growth in skin cancers.

The key to the future of Mankind seems to lie locked inside the powerhouse of the brain. Stimulate it to send the right signals down its fibres and diseases can be cured, paralysis can be ended, behaviour can be changed and life for those in distress or pain can be made pleasant. With medicines and psychiatry a lot can be achieved already. But all people nurse some horror which affects their life and much, much, more could be accomplished at a minor cost; but first barriers, invisible but thick and high and built solidly into the human mind by Man himself, will have to be demolished. The process has begun but it is stupidly slow.

One problem is that corporate action is ruled by vested interests. Thus changes can only be made when vested interests allow. Individuals and nations are encouraged to compete for fame and fortune. So the nations race to reach the South Pole, be the first to climb Everest or to set foot on the moon.

Discoveries and inventions are patented because they can be worth millions of pounds. But many have become an essential part of Man's life in developed countries. Electricity, telephones, radio, television all improve Man's life as well as keeping him much better informed about his world. Great strides are being made in the field of medicine as Man gains a better understanding of himself, both as a race and as individuals.

But, as a species, human beings are incredibly stubborn and insecure. They feel they need to prove to themselves that they are the dominant creatures on earth and within their group that they, personally, are a significant and important part of it. Thus rivalry is born. Man against animal. Man against Man. So far he has used his superior intelligence to establish his supremacy over the world's animal kingdom, dismissing many as insignificant. Even with today's more enlightened attitudes there remains the need to display that superiority by stalking and killing nature's animals with minimal risk to themselves. Indeed it is rare that the animals fight back. In many cases it is their trust which is exploited to bring about their own deaths, and it is only terror which eventually drives them to turn on their attackers only to be met by sophisticated weaponry which the human carries. No human, or group of humans, placed in similar circumstances of being unarmed but facing an armed adversary, could defend themselves and yet the animal, which will turn from trouble unless there is no alternative, is classed as inferior. Man's superiority seems to depend on the instruments of death which he has used his intelligence to develop. Man spends more of the world's resources on death than on life.

Man's rivalry with Man surfaces in many ways and his determination to display his superiority can drive him to lie, cheat and kill. In establishing power and holding it his inhumanity knows no bounds. Unfortunately the human race seems also to have inherited from its ancestors the strong drive to defend its area of habitat against others of the same species. This territorial defence applies to country, town, village or home. It surfaces for example throughout Britain in many ways, from fierce opposition to changes in local environments, such as new housing, or in verbal attacks against the authorities and developers when unused buildings in the area are to be demolished or fields to which the public may have no access are

127

to be built upon. Old, expensive, decrepit and rarely used buildings or churches are defended by people who have never entered their doors. The church authorities themselves may have received a satisfactory settlement which would enable them, if the need was there, to build a new church in the vicinity, yet still local people reject change. It is interesting to see how acceptable building proposals become when the facade, which is the visual message that each member of the public passes to their brain, can be retained while the structure behind is totally demolished and put to different use. The in-built reaction of most humans is to fight change, while there is also the herding or gregarious instincts which pushes them, automaton like, to follow others.

Man responds with the vigour of many animals when his habitat or his way of life are threatened. Skirmish upon skirmish; battle upon battle; war upon war. The older power-ful nations of Europe who colonized many parts of the world, often in the name of Christianity but usually for capital gain, did not always leave behind a legacy of peace within the newly born nations. Many born democratic were soon overthrown by dictatorial megalomaniacs who seized power by the forces of evil and maintained it by terror. Holy wars and crusades undertaken in the name of Christ hundreds of years ago created dual religions in many countries which has resurfaced in waves of killing, maiming and destruction.

Over the ages Man's thoughts and actions have been conditioned by what he has been taught and, until relatively recently, that generally included not questioning their older and wiser teachers. Yet a proper understanding of Man's development on this world has come mainly from those non-conformist, unorthodox individuals who have been prepared to question the teachings of their time. A list of dissidents would include those already mentioned; Copernicus, Kepler, Galileo and Darwin. Despite these wise men, religious teachings have remained virtually unchanged over thousands of years and have played a major part in directing people's thoughts and actions. History however shows that all too often the great power they wielded led either to crushing any opposing views or imposing them, by violence if necessary, on unbelievers. That history is for some reason indelibly etched in the minds of the peoples of the world and is reflected in the religious hatred and fanaticism which drives individuals, groups, and indeed whole nations to inflict inhuman grief and pain on their sworn enemies. Often the hate and consuming terror are directed at members of the same faith but of a different religious persuasion.

Thus, a single race which should form a whole skeleton operating in unison lies in a mass of splintered bones. There are far too many declared specialists, each having a different treatment for his own splinter, but none with the knowledge or ability required to reknit the pieces together and assemble into a working unit.

Today, both inside and outside the church, minds are erupting with question which, for too long, have been bubbling away but contained by society's straitjackets. In much the same way the medical profession has for far too many years refused to accept that ailments could have been helped by treatments outside those which they had been taught, particularly those for which there was no proven scientific basis. Here too the glimmer of reluctant acceptance that alternative medicine can, indeed does, work is brightening. The reluctance remains although minds are adjusting and the new phrase of 'complementary medicine' for this type of treatment is now beginning to give it some long overdue recognition. Osteopathy, homoeopathy, hypnosis and acupuncture are now respectable treatments although still not yet fully accepted by many doctors.

Many people have turned in despair to do-it-yourself medicine, each success bringing a slump in their faith in doctors. The latter seem to have lost the belief that an ounce of reassurance is far greater than a ton of medicine.

Osteopathy is a medical practice which works on the theory that ailments result from structural derangements of bones and muscles which can be corrected by manipulation. Two or three decades ago there were many people suffering backache, particularly slipped discs, who were made by doctors to stay in bed lying on a hard board for weeks on end. Patients in pain, who were prepared to try anything to help, wished to seek relief from osteopaths but were warned by their doctors that such treatment could make matters worse. Many nonetheless turned in desperation to the osteopath. Many were on their feet in a few days.

Homoeopathy is said to be the medical practice of treating like with like. The theory is that the medicine produces the symptoms of the disease being treated in the patient. While doctors take the view that the symptoms come from the illness, homoeopathy sees the symptoms as the body's reaction against the illness as it fights back. The latter therefore stimulates such reaction rather than suppressing it and claims that it treats the patient rather than the disease. There is little doubt that it is effective on many individuals.

Hypnosis is usually only seen in public displays of power by humiliating victims in the atmosphere of a side show. Films too have often portrayed hypnosis as domination of the beautiful by the evil. But it is a very serious method of treatment, one which could help millions of people to improve their lives manyfold. The art of self hypnosis could be taught which could save much anguish and millions of pounds in late treatment. It would need to be properly taught. It would also need to be properly controlled.

Acupuncture is a technique which has been widely practiced by the Chinese for thousands of years although it is only recently that their doctors have been using it very successfully instead of anaesthetics to perform major surgery, including heart operations. The technique is being further developed by using electrical charges through the acupuncture needles to treat many patients with minor problems like grit in the eye to major disorders. In some Far Eastern countries healers practice Yin-Yang which gives them the ability to produce, through their fingertips, different levels of electric power which they use in treating medical cases. It works, but without a scientific basis it remains available in only a few places. In other fields scientists are beginning experiments using magnetism through the acupuncture needles with interesting and exciting developments.

Further research is examining similar concepts to acupuncture, that is where the area being treated is remote from the area with the problem but clearly connected to it through signal carrying nerve ends. One example is that many people get relief from travel sickness by wearing elastic wristbands with a small domed button which presses on an acupuncture spot. They have been remarkably successful for many, preventing sickness from cars to sailing in rough seas. The scope in the field of acupuncture is very wide indeed, yet information to the public is painfully small.

There are many other treatments perhaps less well known, such as phytotherapy, which uses medicinal plants for the treatment of minor illnesses; aromatherapy which, as its names suggests, is the use of sweet smelling oils to influence moods or to treat diseases. To some extent both the examples are already in our daily lives as we eat vegetables for health, or as certain smells, from food to perfumes, excite reaction within us. With the bigotry of the Middle Ages it is very likely that many effective treatments were killed off with those who used them, the latter probably being branded witches and burned at the stake for doing so. But many ancient remedies are still used by individuals today having been passed down from generation to generation. Users often swear by them but because they have no scientific background and, although this applies to modern medicines as well, because they do not work for all people they are derided.

The church itself encourages pilgrims to seek help from their holy shrines and cures, which are achieved at such places, although not understood, are acceptable as acts of God. Such treatments appear to have no scientific basis and thus are not recommended by doctors. But visits to Lourdes come high on the list of places to go for miracle cures and, for some, it works. Many others seek relief from any source, however unlikely, in their desperation for a cure. Wallowing in warm waters, or mud, is popular for reducing pain and there are plenty of plausible, though not scientifically proven, theories why they do.

The wide use of leeches hundreds of years ago has, for many years, been viewed with derision by both the medical profession and public alike as primitive mumbo-jumbo. The reference books refer to this mainly aquatic blood sucking worm being used in the past for medicinal bleeding. Only recently has it been discovered that the leech is in fact a walking chemical factory and that the benefits obtained from its use were from the chemicals it injected into the patient to ease the sucking of the blood and not the actual blood sucking itself. Today the leeches' chemicals have been identified and are regularly used for differing medical uses some, for example, being used in the treatment of heart disorders. Victorian doctors did not question why the leeches worked, but they used them. Maybe there is a lesson to be learned there by today's doctors?

Faith healing is a form of treatment to which the medical profession, who have been taught their trade in universities, remain sceptical. However it too produces relief and cures which cannot be explained. No-one is able to prove whether the claims themselves are true or offer any scientific basis for such claims. Relief or cures could be coincidental or the problem may have been one of the mind rather than the body. It is a field wide open to abuse by money-grabbing quacks whose activities simply cast further doubts in an already misunderstood area of medicine.

Many medical problems are recognized as hereditary, others are yet to be so recognized. There are hundreds of associations scattered around the world involved in raising funds for research into their own particular problem. There is one, sometimes more than one, not only for every part of the body but for several aspects of the mind covering, for example anorexia to schizophrenia; brittle bones to heart diseases; haemophilia to dyslexia; Alzheimer's disease to xenophobia; and for deafness, blindness and paralysis. And with much less public sympathy, associations for the alcoholic, the gambler and the drug addict.

The actions of all animals, both voluntary and involuntary, are controlled from the brain. It is also from this central mind computer that instructions are sent to all parts of the body to swiftly produce the chemicals which, in turn, produce defences against hurt, as well as all feelings such as love, hate, lust, fear, happiness and sorrow. It is also the brain which drives the anorexic towards death and the sexual pervert, the rapist, the killer, the arsonist, to perform their terrible deeds. It is the brain which directs the growth of the body and mind and carries forward problems from generation to generation. Any part of the body whose signal line gets disconnected from the brain is unable to work and becomes paralysed.

So all our reactions are programmed to respond to inputs into the brain: what we see; what we hear; what we eat; what we drink; what we taste; what we inhale; what we smell; what we touch; what touches us; and, those areas where our knowledge is limited, the unseen inputs like radiation.

Once again it seems that all the problems of Mankind are capable of resolution within his own brain and it is here that future research must be concentrated. Like all computers the body computer needs to receive an input before it makes an output. The signals of fear, for example, must reach it before it shoots adrenalin into the bloodstream to alert the human animal to the imminent danger. Faults can arise in the body computer which may cause incorrect signals to be sent out which result in bodily malfunctions or aberrations some of which may drive individuals to crime or other actions against themselves.

Individuals are prisoners of their bodies. Health, feelings, attitudes and behaviour are all pre-set in the genomes of that first fertilized cell. But, as we move to the close of the twentieth century, they are all capable of being changed by cell replacement or by cutting out and replacing genes or parts of genes. Both cell replacement and genetic engineering are on the medical menu today but they are in their infancy and efforts by doctors are being hampered by the moral indignation of those whose thinking has been conditioned by their religious beliefs and who will not try to understand the feelings of sufferers. Thus the moral integrity of doctors has been questioned recently because they replaced damaged brain cells which relieved the great distress of those suffering from Parkinson's disease. When medical research began to indicate that new medicines might allow the use of animal parts to replace defective human parts there were protests, again on moral grounds.

Yet there is great scope for many painful and wretched lives to be made new by brain or body cell replacement and genetic engineering and progress must not be thwarted by such nonsense. The time for shilly-shallying is over and the dead should be required to contribute to life. Such action is being thwarted because entrenched attitudes make it politically very difficult. But if anyone cares for the living then all bodies should, by law, be immediately available to a medical revivification centre for the enhancement of the living. The conditioned thinking ritual, whereby families assemble to watch coffins being lowered into a grave or despatched to the fires of the crematorium, is morbid and only serves to send more pain to the bereaved as the finality of it all is starkly shown. Funerals

133

and stone memorials to the dead in their present form are so much wasted money.

Death of the body is inevitable. It will come to everyone in time. How much better it would be if memorials could consist of a picture, or several pictures, in the family house showing individuals and their families who have been given new life from death. Where tragedies strike bringing large scale deaths a memorial hospital, sports centre, swimming pool, play-ground or other structure useful for the living is far more meaningful than money spent on a stone obelisk. As Christ said: 'Let the dead bury the dead.'

In addition to cell replacement, aberrations could be eliminated by changing the input into the brain to ensure the right output response. It is difficult for those not affected by particular compulsions, obsessions or irresistible impulses, to understand why they are so. In those areas where society is prepared to talk and listen, like anorexia, it is clear that sufferers see the compulsion as a dear friend from whom they derive a great deal of pleasure and comfort. They go to inordinate ends to keep their disease secret simply to avoid it being take from them. It is as necessary to their existence as a drug. They turn to their friend when they are worried, unhappy or under stress and curing them is difficult simply because deep down they do not want to lose that friend. How does the hated rapist, the despised murderer, the loathsome pervert feel? Are they too in the grips of 'friends', fighting in the same way to preserve that friendship?

And what of the men who abuse their own children? Research shows that those fathers who were themselves abused are far more likely to abuse their children than other fathers. It is possible that the problem is hereditary, even jumping a generation or two. Is this another case for which the fiendish friend is responsible?

And how many more maleficent deeds are initiated by this pernicious friend? Indeed is he always pernicious? Although not so much publicized it is certain that people are driven to perform acts of goodness, kindness, love or heroism by compulsions. Even normal activities like exercise can become addictive. Whatever the truth the anathema seems to hover at the start of a mental culvert, opening the sluice gates whenever it will, causing the driving force to flow until the act is done.

The fiends in the horror stories and films, which most people were brought up on, nearly always became active on the night of a full moon. Whilst such stories may remain a myth it is surprising how many millions of people believe there is some correlation between the moon, planets and stars and individuals. People read the horoscopes in newspapers more than any other part. During the 1980s America's President Reagan used astrology, and opponents quoted that to cast doubts on his abilities or mental state. But without innuendo no-one could prove he was wrong to do so. It is another of those areas wide open to abuse and, because it is little understood and because the information about it is inadequate, it is too often dismissed as a joke. It is known and accepted that tides are produced in the oceans by magnetic forces, so why is it doubted that those changes in force fields made by the earth's movement in the solar system can affect life on earth?

Every individual on earth is different. For many years now he has been identified by his unique fingerprints but new methods are being discovered. The latest is called genetic fingerprinting where an individual can be identified by his genes which are present in every part of his body. Thus a hair, fragment of skin or body fluid, carries his unique genetic signature. Would it really be any loss of freedom if, at birth, such unique details were recorded and stored for comparative purposes. Surely that would protect only the innocent. It could also remove the dreadful trauma of the need to identify the bodies of loved ones and thus preserve happy memories.

But progress has yet to be made on identifying the unique cosmic force field which each individual carries – aura. Such a magnetic field would interact with other force fields and become one of the sources of signal input to the brain producing feelings, reactions, drive, healing, and projections. As with all magnetic fields it would have its twin poles, with like repelling and unlike attracting. Thus, person to person reactions can produce an instant and inexplicable dislike of someone at the first meeting or can drive normally resolute people to become slaves to masters who exploit, hurt and abuse them. Other non-personal reactions can be seen to bring an irrational fear of a particular house or building which hits some people as soon as they cross the threshold.

Differing illnesses may have their own characteristic force

135

field signature which reacts with antagonistic fields and activates the dormant disease. The study of force fields should enable individuals to identify the magnetic lines which are antagonistic to them. Such identification may help in detecting and dealing with those magnetic fields which may lead to unprovoked violence and crime.

Compulsions, urges or feelings may be brought on as the sun rises or sets, by the moon in its phases, or by the stars. Many people now may identify their cycle of life. Tiredness, alcohol or drugs will reduce the normal ability of individuals to fight off persistent drives caused by antagonistic force fields. And the powerhouse brain is as much underused as it is little understood. But even in its subconscious state the brain can excite the force fields to output signals. Sometimes these signals can be detected by others. Sometimes, particularly in times of great fear or trauma, they are absorbed and retained in other receptive fields around them to be reproduced to a passing receptive mind field. The silent scream of fear emanating in signals! Ghosts!

But the powerhouses can also be affected by the invisible magnetic lines which run across countries, creating changing patterns of powerful forces. And in many countries force fields are dropping from overhead electrical cables or from the vast number of electrical and electronic equipment such a televisions, videos, fridges, freezers, audio equipment, cookers, washing machines, mixers, cleaners, hair dryers, lamps, drills, mowers and computers. And within their differing local habitats humans are generating their own individual force fields which interact with those around them. It is impossible within present knowledge to know whether such interaction causes health or behavioural problems because each person would react differently.

It is no use flinching with horror or moral indignation at the thought that actions can be changed through brain cell replacement, genetic engineering or other methods of changing signals to the brain. Already hormone injections are used to replace those which the brain normally produces but have stopped for some reason. Mankind has the tools and must now begin to use them to improve the lives of those in distress and pain, to eliminate hereditary illnesses, and to eradicate violent

136

crime. For he has reached a crossroad in his development and must now decide whether he will continue to allow his world to be dominated by a tiny minority of evil people whose religion is death.

The human race, using its latest knowledge, can treat those whose actions bring grief and distress to others by compulsory medical treatment using cell and gene changes, or by the input of signals into the brain to bring a changed response. Such treatment would be far better than incarceration, particularly if the crime were that they are unable to refuse a 'friend'. Because everyone does not have a persistent 'friend', such people who do should not be regarded as weak. On the contrary it could be argued that their single minded determination towards self destruction is a strength far greater than the ordinary. However it is viewed, help whether wanted or not, must be given. Punishment becomes irrelevant.

Anger about rapists who commit sadistic violations on weaker innocent victims, in many cases virtually destroying their lives, has prompted strident calls for the perpetrators to be castrated. Medical opinion is that this would not remove the driving force to stop the horrors being committed again. But such calls demonstrate that there must be an end to legal attempts to deal with the problem by punitive means. It is getting worse and there is a growing demand for some medical action to be taken to curb it.

Certain cases can be examined now and those belong to the people whose secret is out. Included in this area are those who are bent on their own suicidal paths and those who have been found guilty of heinous crimes against humanity. In both cases cell replacements, genetic changes or brain signal input to change responses must be considered. They must be excellent alternatives in the case of those individuals who are pushing themselves towards death where all other treatments are failing. And dealing with vicious criminals this way would not only calm the calls for the death penalty but could be considered a better alternative to it. Once the treatments are proven the problems would emerge and could be treated. Only thus will the exponential growth of violence be stopped.

Every generation criticizes 'the kids of today' usually accompanied by the expression 'in my day'. But there is little doubt that the world is becoming ever more violent. In the first half of the century a murder would be headlined in every paper; today they are so common they hardly rate more than a paragraph or two tucked away in the middle pages. Killings have become more senseless and definitely more brutal. Old people are attacked and killed with no apparent motive. The small sums of money involved in robberies would not, to a stable person, be a motive for killing. Women are abducted from estate agents, trains, motorways and are attacked in their own beds at home. Children are abducted from their homes, while playing nearby, shopping or on paper rounds. Old people are attacked and beaten to death, the women often raped beforehand. All demonstrate the unhealthy increase in violence. People living in some areas of cities are ruled by mobs who are known to them. They may see brutality, they may see death, but they can only speak anonymously for they are aware of what the ruling mob can, and will, do to them.

Even non-residents who may see crimes or violence are warned by the kindly locals to ignore what they have seen. Why risk your life, or that of your family, over someone elses troubles? Not only does it not help to put a stop to such mob power but it encourages it to greater violence. But life is not so cheap and society cannot ask people to place themselves and, worse, their families in a position of constant, nagging fear. The law cannot be enforced without the evidence. The evidence will not be forthcoming until the fear is removed. But fear is like a forest fire, unchecked it will bring devastation. Today 'forest fears' are burning in many inner cities and only when they are tackled by society will the extent of the human damage emerge. Whilst the forces of evil are allowed to flourish unhindered more and more people will lose their individual freedom. Where are the human rights activists? The few must not rule the many.

Before proper treatment can be given Man needs to get the truth, the whole truth and nothing but the truth. Oaths amongst those prepared to kill are meaningless. Playing a game with words must cease. The protection of evil must cease. With Man's advanced knowledge today it is not beyond him to devise a system, or group of systems, which will ensure that he gets the truth. But it may be beyond his vested interests. For everyone likes to keep secret some things and tell lies about others. But truth must be obtained if Man is to survive, for truth is freedom, truth is love, truth is immortality.

The goal is deity.

10

'Today,' said the wise man, 'is the beginning of tomorrow.'

And that must be Mankind's springboard to the future. For, as with every personal tragedy, everything behind the present moment has happened, gone into history to be dispersed in due course by the mists of time. What matters is the way forward, the now yet to come.

Today therefore is the time for every human being on the planet to look into his own life and question once again what he personally is doing here and why. To do so he must reach deep within himself, to see how his past has been shaped by conditioned thinking which has ruled not only his life thus far but those of his ancestors for many centuries. Are they appropriate for today? More importantly are they appropriate for tomorrow?

In setting the patterns of Man's past, religion has played a major role, but somewhere along the line it seems to have lost its original message in a welter of humans grasping for power and indulging in rituals which have assumed greater importance than the message itself. The lives and philosophies of key figures of history were recorded in the sacred writings of the world's major religions, although none of those figures wrote anything themselves. Indeed their philosophies and teachings were written by scholars well after the events in terms which the writers could understand and which were therefore affected by their life and times. But for the scriptures to be alive to contemporary generations their interpretations must be revised again and again to keep abreast of current knowledge. Such revisions must always, always, look to the future of Mankind and not to the future of a religion.

Taking a look at today's religions, the oldest monotheistic, belief in one God, is Judaism and in its early form was fundamental to both Christianity and Islam. The concept of

God, and heaven and hell which he will use to reward or punish as appropriate, is an integral theme of the three religions.

Christianity acknowledges Jesus Christ as its founder and every variety of the many Christian denominations claim him as their authority in one way or another. The early Christians believed that God had acted decisively for the salvation of the world. The new religion was based on his teachings, with the key centre point of his death and resurrection. Christianity was first organized as a movement within Judaism and the early Christian Jews maintained that the sole difference between the two religions was the acknowledgement that Jesus was the Messiah and they expected, and demanded, that the heathen converts obey the laws of Moses. But Christianity was advanced by its preachers as a universal religion, and it was taken to the gentiles where it rapidly spread through the Mediterranean area. The Jews themselves, after years of oppression, had grasped more firmly to the hope of a Messiah who would rid them of the rule of both Romans and high priests, and saw Christ's teachings as antagonistic to their national or political aims. The disagreement is set out in the Bible in Hebrews which is often seen as the first recorded apology of Christianity. It exhorts Christians not to return to Judaism under the pressure of persecution.

Jewish Christianity remained dominant until the Jerusalem church was dispersed shortly before the destruction of Jerusalem itself in 70 AD, after which the Jewish influence diminished rapidly. Christian history shows all too clearly how religions can be tinkered with by Man. Today Christianity flourishes in literally hundreds of differing beliefs, rituals and policies over which oceans of blood have been, and continue to be, spilt.

By the seventh century when Mohammed founded the Islamic religion (now considered to be the fastest growing religion) Christian and Jewish missionaries had secured many converts from the pagan ranks. Unlike Christ, Mohammed was seen only as a messenger of God. He taught that the creator of the universe ruled with great love and mercy, and submission to his will without question was essential in his followers. They were required to surrender themselves, and those whose lives they count as dearer than their own, unconditionally and totally to the will of God. The Islamic religion regards this unfolding of God's revelation to Mankind as a complete system of faith and behaviour whose prototype is preserved in heaven with God. They regard as imperfect the earlier versions of the revelations given to Christian and Jew.

The Koran, the sacred book of Islam, is regarded as the word of God as revealed to Mohammed by the angel Gabriel. It was compiled after the death of Mohammed and, to some extent, was derived from the Jewish scriptures. In the early days Mohammed was friendly with Christian and Jew, indeed there was recognition of the Old Testament prophets and Christ. But the fiery zealots who had brought in the hard line, like the Christian with the Jews, coerced and persecuted unbelievers. The main sects of Sunnites and Shiites follow beliefs and practices which not only vary but often are antagonistic.

It is interesting to wonder why three of the major religions of the world were born in the same small geographical corner.

Further eastward, Brahmanism worshipped a supreme deity. It taught that from Brahma's head sprang the holy Brahman, that is those who established themselves as custodians and makers of the law. Of inferior birth were princes and warriors who were said to come from the arms of Brahma. Further down the chain were the farmers who came from the maker's thighs, and the Sudra, the artisans and labourers, from his feet. The rest of Mankind were outcasts. Thus the origin of the caste system, which can be seen today, was born. In contact with contemporary faith and modes of thought Brahmanism ran to seed through indecent practices, eventually emerging into a complex system of theology called Hinduism.

Hinduism is polytheistic having three Gods, seen as a trinity, with Brahma the creator, Vishnu the preserver, and Siva the destroyer, each being worshipped by his own devotees. The religious thought separating them is as wide as the gulf dividing Roman Catholic from Protestant, or Sunnite from Shiite.

It was a Hindu who, some five centuries before Christ, established the Buddhist faith. The arrogance of the priesthood and the injustices of the caste system were crying evils in Buddha's time. He made no attempt to solve the origins of Man but proclaimed equality and brotherhood. Buddhism recognizes no soul, and therefore no after life, but sees actions and thoughts as irrevocable and irredeemable. Such thoughts and actions retain an inexplicable existence until they had been rewarded or punished. The life of an insect is considered as precious as a man's. Celibacy led to monks and nuns establishing the seats of knowledge in monasteries and, imperceptibly, the priestly supremacy and arrogance which Buddha worked so hard to overthrow was re-established. Buddha wrote nothing and it took a hundred years before his philosophies were reduced to the written word. Over the years the beliefs were absorbed into other faiths and Buddhism too is rent with deep gulfs.

But his original basic principles hold a great attraction to many millions of people in today's world. Like Buddha himself, they feel that religions generally have become a recitation of rituals and beliefs; the former often without meaning or compassion, the latter contaminating the human race with hatred, invective, bloody violence and senseless killings.

Long before all these religions, fetishism ruled, the common practice in which various inanimate objects were regarded as imbued with life and power and consequently were revered. Such a practice was inevitable in primitive superstitious minds which believed a hidden magic lay in such things as charms, animals' teeth and bones, or other amulets which gave the carrier extraordinary powers. Thus the objects were seen as tools in the hands of Man for him to command as they would a genie.

The worship of idols, images and icons followed, believing that they represented the deity or other supernatural beings who commanded nature's actions whether in providing food, helping to win battles, or bringing the life-saving rain or death-dealing earthquakes. This worship was quite different from fetishism as the deity was a being superior to the worshippers. It was not long before that difference was exploited and they became tools of power for religious leaders to use to further their own ends.

In their fight against heathenism the early Christians forbade the introduction of images or pictures into churches as they savoured too much of idolatry. Over hundreds of years the arguments raged until they were eventually admitted, but with a distinction carefully drawn between adoration and reverence, only the latter being allowed and then not to the images themselves but to the persons they represented. The practice of

143

using images to help devotion grew rapidly and candles and incense were offered to them. But the opponents argued successfully that fetishism had crept into the use of images and they were banned for some years before they returned again. Today's Roman Catholic church strongly supports the use of images.

And through many thousands of years and many new religions fetishism has maintained a strong hold on Man, until today, all over the world, millions and millions of people have their own inanimate objects which they believe have the power to safeguard them and bring them good fortune. Some may be small enough to carry in the pocket, some look for their magic in a building or from a tree. There are those who wish on the moon, even more on the stars. There are hundreds of thousands of fetishes practiced daily by many religious people which involve a conglomerate of holy magic. Images and places are given aural powers from which worshippers try to draw divine wisdom or strength. So fetishism is without doubt the most widely practiced ritual in the world knowing no barriers of caste, class or education. It is practiced by the most primitive people and the most sophisticated in the world. It has flourished in the different guises of totemism, taboo, ju-ju, voodoo, witchcraft and superstition.

In the Christian religion there is the Turin shroud. Sadly, scientists removed a lot of its magic by proving it came from a much later period. But for many it will retain its aura of reverence, partly because it has been associated with Christianity for hundreds of years and partly because of its age. Age means ghosts. Ghosts of bygone days, of yesterday, of today, sometimes visible, mostly not, but present, without doubt, present.

Within all Man's religions and beliefs there is an interweaving of related principles such as the belief in the sanctity of life, at least of human life. Yet in our world today the differences between the religions are a major cause of the sickening growth of indiscriminate slaughter over the recent decades. But in its presentation there is no democracy in religion, for it is argued that it is God's instructions to Man. Too often, however, the strong beliefs and passions of individuals can over-ride sanity. Pity Mankind when that happens.

It is inevitable that those who compiled the sacred writings in all faiths would have interpreted the teachings in their own way, such that they would have been coloured by contemporary and local conditions and customs, as well as containing the *bete noire* of the religious leaders of the time. Thus, in varying degrees, faiths have denounced theft, deception, the use of intoxicants, alongside incontinence and unchastity. Some faiths discourage marriage amongst those spreading the gospel while others forbid it. Some preach polygamy. Some that the cow is holy, the pig unclean. To one faith every form of life on earth is important, to another the world's animal and plant life was provided solely for Man to do with as he wishes. To some there is life after death, to others there is none. Some faiths teach their followers that the most worthy and sure way to heaven is by giving their lives in suicidal attempts against the enemy, they being defined by religious leaders claiming to be speaking on behalf of God.

However it has grown, Man has planted the tree of internecine death which flourishes with branches spread all over Mankind and roots tunnelling their way towards the destruction of Man's planet. The vast majority of humankind want to live in peace and to build a world that will provide a sound and terror-free future for their children and their children's children. Many, many, millions of ordinary people gave their lives in two world wars ostensibly for just those reasons. Unless Mankind acts, not only nationally but internationally, to deal effectively with the tiny minorities which are controlling street, town and country by fear and intimidation, their sacrifices will have been in vain. It was a massive tragedy that the young people of the world were required to die in wars in the first place. It would be an unforgivable travesty if they died for nothing.

Hope surfaced in the 1960s with the flower power movement which preached love. If it did nothing else it stirred Man's conscience and disturbed his apathy. It created a momentum against racial discrimination. It brought people peacefully demonstrating on the streets against the stupidity and futility of war. But the spontaneous gestures and philosophies were hijacked by vested interest. The movement became the foundation for drugs as they were freely promoted to dull the senses, ease pain and sorrow, and remove inhibitions. Drug abuse with stimulants, hallucinogens and narcotics took many into a downward spiral of death while creating a massively lucrative business for those dealing in degradation. Politicians too used the movement wherever possible to publicize their personal politics. So flower power was wafted away into a waterfall of indifference, its name sullied.

But the aroused consciences caused people to begin to look more closely at their world and question the actions of their governments. It brought to the fore Man's embezzlement of his declared birthright, his world and its animal inhabitants. It resulted in efforts being made to save the surprisingly high number of endangered species. This situation had been brought about by Man going too often to the well for furs, skins, or food and to satisfy his need to prove himself by killing for sport. Those efforts succeeded in changing society's thinking, and furs and skins went out of fashion. But that destroyed those communities whose livelihoods had relied upon that trade for hundreds of years.

But those sort of problems were ignored by society and what should have been a world affair was left to national governments to sort out. However, although progress has been much slower, on their own governments have found some ways to help and their successes show. Today for example the horrific pictures of Man clubbing baby seals to death is muted as the practice has been rigidly controlled or outlawed. But can we in Europe complain at the people of Peru who, because their usual fishing has been seriously affected, are turning to dolphins to provide food unless we are offering an alternative?

The control of culling seals is an example of how cross-nation humanity can work to effect changes. But there is a need for a world organization which is funded to protect the world and its environment. It is unreasonable to expect the poor to abandon ways of raising money for food simply because they are a danger to the planet. Few of them will have heard of the ozone layer. Few will understand how their actions are causing the greenhouse effect. None will understand why we are asking them to accept poverty, starvation or death. It is really unfortunate for them that their contribution to the destruction of the environment began at a time when the problems have just been highlighted. For they have grown from centuries of pollution from every organized nation of the world. So we must recognize that the problems are the world's and the issue is the

146

future of Mankind.

So there is a need to appeal to all of us to lower the drawbridges which we have pulled up on life, to forget the political and religious dogma which has been forced upon us by many years of conditioned thinking, to forget national and local pride and prejudices and look towards a future which our current attitudes and ideas will shape. The vulnerable must be protected. The future of Mankind must be protected. Justice should not only be done, but should manifestly and undoubtedly be seen to be done.

At every turn Man takes, at every crossroad he reaches, for every future problem facing him he needs the truth. His laws are geared to protect the guilty because he is afraid to infringe on the liberty of the innocent. The result is exactly the opposite. Many countries are being faced with minority groups of unnamed people bringing disorder and economic ruin by threatening violence to the tradesmen, officials of government and transport workers by coercion through intimidation. The removal of the right to remain silent will be fought by activists wherever it is suggested. Why? Who does it protect? Not the innocent; not the uninvolved; not the fearful; not the vulnerable. Such matters must be for the people themselves to decide and not powerful minority groups, even when the latter covers governments.

And what is special about Man? What is it which leads him to believe that he has the right to do exactly as he wishes regardless of other inhabitants of the planet? Indeed are the actions being driven out of his control by the failure of his leaders to defend his freedom?

Certainly Man has many unusual features compared with earth's other mammals. He walks upright on his hind legs; his brain is large; his face flattened with a prominent turned down nose; his skin is covered with millions of microscopic sweat glands giving him an ability to sweat which is unmatched in apes. Above all he is unique in being able to think. His brain has the ability to assimilate information so that he can decide which is the best way forward for him. But can he? Is he really free to choose? Are an individual's actions not constrained by what he has been taught and by what is going on in his own world?

There is in each individual an internal biological clock

which is programmed to react throughout life. Meal times, bed times are daily examples, the menstruation cycle a monthly one. But for many that clock also dictates the manner of death as well as of living. Its signals make the body vulnerable to the dormant inherited diseases. Its signals bring puberty and the menopause. Its signals bring senility. Its signals bring death. In a way that can be seen only by individuals, or sometimes family members, its signals bring back the attitudes of parents or grandparents in moodiness, in gestures, in actions, in temper tantrums, in stubbornness.

And we should all remember that every single member of our race spends nearly one third of his life in an extremely vulnerable position. For those who reach the three score years and ten will have spent twenty-three years of their lives asleep, when they are blind, deaf and paralysed. For in sleep the brain remains active, carrying out its life support activities, but it disconnects itself from the usual signal inputs of the eyes, the ears and the muscles. No-one really knows what the brain does during that time but one thing is certain, it is dealing with its programmed instructions and not those that the individual would wish to pass on through his conscious mind. Work, rest, play, are all controlled and the rhythm of life links Man to all the animals with which he shares the world.

Man has come a long way in the twentieth century and if the recent rate of progress continues he could, unless he acts quickly, find himself unready when, in the not too distant future, he reaches the ultimate moral dilemma when he knows that he can achieve the power to recall his memory in a newly born baby and thus will be able to create immortality for himself.

Before that happens it is absolutely essential that he can establish truth, for with it the world will be a simpler and better place where crimes could be unwound by straight-forward questioning, where there would be no legal wriggling and no need for years of investigation to prove guilt or innocence. For major crimes at least there would be no need for esoteric arguments on the meaning of each separate word in the law as there is today. All of us at some time in our lives have come across different meanings to words than those we were used to. Reference to the dictionary is not the answer either as meanings of words do change with new generations. Laws are

148

needed as simple as the Commandments themselves but they must be regularly revised and updated to take account of society's changes. Only thus will Lord Hewart's extremely wise words on justice be fulfilled, and unless they are then anarchy and disaster will befall all of us. We are sliding that way and we must act to stop it. Now is the time.

To find the way of truth, which is the only way to make Man free, it is necessary to extricate our minds from our in-built attitudes and our conditioned opposition to change. We will have to lower those drawbridges and go out of our limited circle of family and friends and begin to act as members of the human family. And this means if we do not like our fellow human family members we should do something about them and not just ignore them hoping they will go away. Over many centuries many leading political figures have joined religious leaders to pay homage at the altar of truth but none have seen it as a finite requirement, for a world where truth is king could be a very uncomfortable world indeed!

But I cannot accept that Man, with all his present technology, is unable to produce a system which can distinguish lie from truth even though, to satisfy everyone, it may need to involve a whole series of checks and counterchecks. How much longer can the human race continue to act in its primitive tribal way? How much longer are the vast majority prepared to allow painful and sickening suffering to strike millions of people? There can be no distinction between those who are experiencing hell on earth, which appears to have been afflicted upon them, from those who appear to have self-inflicted their own pain. Neither are able to help themselves, only others can do so.

Man needs the truth to survive. Whatever God individuals may believe in, nature has provided Mankind with power within himself which can be used for good or evil and there remain many, many wonders yet to unfold. But it is senseless to allow ingrained beliefs to compel inaction while awaiting for some divine intervention. Mankind is on his own. He can be absolutely certain that he will have to solve the problems of his world, many of which he has created himself. The use of nationalism to inflame passions to violence must stop. Territorial instincts must be quashed. Before punitive actions are taken they must be measured in human degradation terms. No arms,

149

no wars. No wars, no genocide. The majority interest must prevail, particularly by dealing with the few who are ruling the masses by terror and intimidation.

Only thus will that most basic of human rights, freedom from fear, be given to all people of the world. We must encourage the development and introduction of medicinal engineering to treat and cure violent criminals, which will always be more effective than vengeful punishment. Terror, no matter what banner it hides under, must be rooted out by every human being regardless of race, colour or creed. Priests or other confidantes should offer no succour to the violent. No longer can anyone justify allowing those committing acts of fear or terror to wander freely in society. They too need treatment. But, in all cases, those in need of help must be able to go somewhere to get it and not simply be incarcerated. No one will volunteer for that.

The richer developed nations must help the younger and poorer nations. In much the same way that children come of age and insist on learning by their own mistakes, so too do the child-nations. Trying to be an overhelpful parent nation simply aggravates the problems. But the offer of help must always be open. There needs to be an understanding that even in the 1990s there are extremely wide differences in Man's standards of living around the globe, varying from remote tribes living a Stone Age existence through to groups and countries of great affluence. So before condemning actions by the poorer nations which are harming the environment those countries with longer histories should look back on how their own actions started the problems.

In almost every part of the world new nations, and older ones tackling the problems of poverty, are going through the same development curves that todays affluent nations went through hundreds or thousands of years ago but with one major difference – international politics. The saying is often true, that generally people do not know how badly off they are until some well-meaning person tells them. This brings unrest which fuels riots. Add politics and sophisticated weaponry as the torch to the fuel and an explosion of chaos and death results.

Looking back many centuries Britain used to be heavily forested. More recently its industrial revolution poured carbon

150

gases into the atmosphere which added to the developing greenhouse effect. It is only forty years ago that people in major British cities were dying directly from the thick impenetrable combination of fog, and smoke from chimneys as coal was burnt. Today Scandinavia is blaming Britain's coal-burning emissions into the atmosphere for the acid rain which has produced a slow death for many of their forests.

When it comes to wars Britain has had its share of internal wars as the powerful factions fought to be rulers of the country. There was a succession of wars between Protestant and Catholic monarchs. Would the politicians have acted the way they did in 1688 when they invited the Protestant William III, Prince of Orange, to become King of England and overthrow the Catholic James II at the Battle of Boyne in 1690, had they known that the anger and hatred fomented would have kept that battle going for three hundred years? Would the Crusaders, who went to recover the Holy Land from the Moslems time and time again over three centuries, think that their efforts were worthwhile given the chaotic situation which exists in that area today, some seven centuries later? And English history is full of kings quelling revolting peasants. How different would history have been had some interfering nation provided the peasants with armour and training to match the monarch's forces?

But all the while over hundreds of years democracy has developed and at the beginning of the twentieth century so much of the world had been colonized by Britain that it proudly boasted that the sun never set on the British Empire. But Britain was only one of the European countries that had been through the same historical growing pains and which had colonies all over the world.

People who have learned from their own past errors must realize that their children reach a stage where they too can only learn by their mistakes. To them advice can be given, but not criticism.

And what about wealth and power? There is something terribly indecent about the extravagances of wealth whilst millions of people are dying of malnutrition. Of course wealth is an incentive to us all but some of the sums reported to be paid, such as tens of millions of pounds to one person for one film, does seem excessive. And there are many other similar

151

instances. But wealth can be said to be comparative and it could be argued that it is just as indecent to own houses, cars or the trappings of the society in which we live. While fellow humans are dying of neglect how can we, as Christians, justify the many millions of pounds which we spend in the celebration of Christ's birthday on food, drink and presents. How can we justify the thousands of millions more spent on adornments of gold and jewels? Can anyone argue that such actions are not also indecent? Given the will, disease and hunger can be eradicated from the world by the people of the richer nations helping the poor. Such help must exclude, most emphatically, the provisions of war, regardless of the politics of the receiving State. It can be done and you and I can do it.

Some concern for the future has emerged during the 1980s as many political parties begin to adopt the environmental policies of Green politics. But we must look beyond Man's rape of his environment to the massive atrocities he is committing, or allowing to be committed, against the vulnerable members of his own race. Crucial to the future of Man should be the fundamental principle of a *Life First* philosophy, but that philosophy must mean *life* and not just living. We must seek to achieve, as the prime objective of all governments, the protection and enrichment of all human life. With such a philosophy no-one should be forced to suffer great pain or unbearable indignity when there is no hope of relief. That is not life, but a living death. Thousands of lives can be save by eradicating killer diseases in poorer nations as they have in the affluent countries.

And we must begin to realize, accept and embrace, that our love is given to living beings and our love is sustained by our memories of them. Dead bodies are not the persons we loved so dearly for, whether you have a religion or not, the spirit has gone from them and all that is left is but a lifeless mass. How better could we show our love for them than by making their bodies work in the same generous spirit as they would have in life, in a useful and caring way. By giving their empty bodies we could end the despair of those praying for someone to grant life to their dying wives, husbands, sweethearts, parents or children.

In both these ways we have the power to play God for we have the power to give life. Surely we can no longer deny life to

152

those who need it particularly in the practices of burning or burying our dead?

We must also provide help to the poorer nations to enable Mankind to solve the problems of the planet itself – holes in the ozone layer; the greenhouse effect; and pollution on land, sea and in the air from chemicals and effluent. In the 1990s all political parties are having to adopt the environmental policies of the Green party and begin to allocate funds towards repairing the damage that Man has inflicted on his planet and its environment. Only money can stop further deterioration. Only by helping the proletariat of poor States by giving massive and regular help on a planned basis, can any recovery work.

But continuing hand-outs are not enough for Man needs to develop a purpose in life. In those regions of the world where death from hunger has been around for thousands of years there is a crying need for a properly planned international approach to end this unnecessary suffering by artificial methods of altering inhospitable environments. I am convinced that most people of the world are caring people with perhaps too many of them enveloped in their own problems. But they can elect governments which can be charged with dealing with these problems even if it means a 'charity tax'. In the meantime the governments of the more affluent nations must provide sufficient resources to the starving nations simply to maintain life at all.

Each of us must look within ourselves to recognize that it is Man's approach to life on his planet, yours and mine, which itself is driven by what lies within us, which has caused the problems. The knowledge which Man has, as this century draws to its close, is sufficient to begin the recovery which will ensure his future. But he needs to understand and fight those knee-jerk reactions which lie within him. Look at his behaviour over the Salman Rushdie book, *The Satanic Verses*. It is clearly deeply offensive to the Moslems who are an extremely devout people. For the sake of peace in the world, for the sake of the living, for the sake of healing hatred, why could not the book simply be withdrawn and destroyed? Compensation could have been paid. Yet so many eminent people rushed to defend its publication, arguing that freedom of expression was essential. But there are few countries, if any, which will permit

153

inflammatory literature to be freely published. Attacks against black people, Jews, or others who may stand out in a crowd is offensive to most of us and is quite rightly banned. Ask those people who were living in peace with the Moslems what has happened to their freedom from fear as a result of Rushdie's book.

The reactive force field which the book produced demonstrates how, sadly to me at least, the word 'respect' has disappeared from the English language as books, films, and television have conditioned the thinking of the young by ridiculing every pillar which holds their society together. Politicians may be fair game for that but is it necessary, or acceptable, to take cruel digs at their personal features or habits such as speech defects or other impediments? Are the writers themselves attacked in this way? Is their work accepted or rejected according to their personal features or habits? Neither God nor Jesus Christ have escaped the crude sideswiping. Such attacks not only demoralizes, they add nothing to Man's life or world except grief, while they successfully push further away the achievement of peace and tolerance. Freedom of expression cannot mean freedom from responsibility and thus cannot be defended as one of the rights of Man. God preserve Mankind from well-meaning people.

It is important in life to recognize and accept that youth needs to have its fling of freedom. It is brief, it is wonderful, and troubles will come soon enough.

The jury system of justice has had doubts cast upon it and I can understand that as one sees how the law practitioners play at their own esoteric game. But I can see many benefits in introducing equalizers, selected like jurists at random, to become the guardians of major national policies for, far too often, so called debates in parliament are window dressing and politicians vote the way they are told. We are all aware the division bell brings many members of parliament, absent during the whole debate, to vote. One such vote took enormous power out of the hands of elected representatives of the trades union movement and, under the banner of greater democracy, required a ballot to be taken before certain events were legal. Interesting to think what might happen if governments were required to follow a similar procedure with a representative jury! The idea raises the question of whether an elected government is there to provide what the people want or what they think the people should be made to have.

But with the earth being only one infinitesimal part of a gigantic universe with every single one of its billions of planets, stars, comets or meteorites all tied together in some massive scientific rule book, no-one can deny that some form of supernatural power exists. And this tiny planet and all the plant and animal life it holds are tied to the same cosmic and nuclear structure as the rest of the universe. Man calls that power God but religion has taught him to tie that powerful God to historic figures. Thus the Christians believe that Jesus Christ was the son of that God born onto this planet to save Mankind. But the religion which followed and is said to be based on his teachings was formed when ordinary Man believed earth was the centre of the universe. Today we can see that in comparison with the controlling power of the universe, Jesus was but a mortal. That he was here there is no doubt. That he was an important visitor with something to say there is no doubt. The question is was his visit in vain? Has Man paid any attention at all to what he was actually saying? He obviously wanted Mankind to listen but somewhere vested interests have produced religious interpretations. Before it's too late, for God's sake, for your own sake, for pity's sake, reject these interpretations and read what he actually said and did to try to influence Man's life upon earth.

And then begin to understand that your future, and that of your descendants, will depend upon your actions.

Our first and most difficult move will be to fight our addiction to the drug of materialism. We can no longer pretend not to notice the plight of our fellow human beings. Our lives were made uncomfortable by being reminded of the slaughter of animals so that we could wear fur coats, and society changed. It could change again if, for example, we measured our personal adornments in human lives. On us they are but the trappings of status symbols; in the hands of the poor they can, at the very least, deny the Grim Reaper his harvest.

Are we going to listen to the pitiful cries of those communities facing death from malnutrition? Are we going to demand changes in our society so that we may grant life to the dying? Are we going to stand up and demand that we rid the world of those inhuman, vicious people who terrorize the vulnerable.

The last year of the 1980s will fill many pages of the history books. But they will not be able to capture, or perhaps even understand, the scenes of whole nations crying tears of joy as though some heavy weight has been lifted from them. For the world can look back on twelve exciting months in which impossible dreams began to come true. One man, Mikhael Gorbachev, almost singlehandedly, began releasing the shackles of tyranny bringing an outflow of freedom to all the nations of Eastern Europe, culminating in the destruction of the much hated wall separating East and West Berlin. But there are signs that opportunists are threatening his plans and undermining his authority. What a tragedy it would be if such ill-considered power grasping wrecked such a man of history.

And, also in 1989, in South Africa another man took, at long last, the first faltering steps towards abolishing the anachronistic policy of apartheid.

Leaders in both countries have a long way to go, having to battle against overwhelming opposition from the powerful factions that have held sway for so long in their countries. They need recognition for what they are doing as well as moral and financial support from all free peoples if they are to succeed. The wheel of freedom is turning but to remove the brakes too quickly can only end in a crash. We must press all those who have waited so long to curb their natural impatience for speedy changes. For the leaders must have time to succeed. Praying for success is not enough, every one of us must do all we can to help, for if they fail the human race fails and we will all have to take a share of the blame. Above all we must not allow, yet again, rabid nationalists or religious fanatics to spoil the best chance the world has ever had for lasting peace. Such opportunities are rare. Time after time mankind has failed to act to grasp them. He may never have another opportunity like this one.

And so, as the world moves towards the end of the twentieth century, Man has the ability to give life to millions by putting an end to death by starvation and those diseases for which he already has the cures. He must abandon his inbuilt squeamishness about his own body, he must give up his dead for life and he must allow the specialists to deal with those inherited traits which are making his life a misery. The latter means the use of both genetic engineering and cell replacement both to cure

156

illnesses as well as to treat violent and persistent criminals. He must look to international joint ventures in research and stop competing with himself. And he must look for ways to help the poor in order to preserve his planet. For Earth is the planet of Man and only he can protect it and its inhabitants. The opportunity is there. The ability is there. Has he got the will? Dammit Man, are you never going to learn? Are you never going to stop reacting and begin to solve your problems? The time is well overdue for you to take charge of your own destiny for, no matter how you look at it, and no matter how much you may not like it, you have no choice.